MICHAEL DOUGLAS

MICHAEL DOUGLAS

A Biography

ALAN LAWSON

WARNER BOOKS

A *Warner* Book

First published in Great Britain
in 1993 by Robert Hale

This edition published by Warner Books in 1994

Copyright © Alan Lawson 1993

The moral right of the author has been asserted

A CIP catalogue record for this book
is available from the British Library

ISBN 0 7515 0851 9

Photoset in North Wales by
Derek Doyle & Associates, Mold, Clwyd
Printed and bound in Great Brtain by
Clays Ltd, St Ives plc

Warner Books
A division of
Little, Brown and Company (UK) Limited
Brettenham House
Lancaster Place
London WC2E 7EN

Contents

This book is dedicated
to all those who dare not sleep
because they fear the dawn

Illustrations

A youthful Michael Douglas in *Hail Hero!* (1969)

The aggressive young actor in *Coma* (1978)

Karl Malden and Michael Douglas on the *Streets of San Francisco* (1972)

Michael Douglas with Jack Lemmon and Jane Fonda in *The China Syndrome* (1979)

Michael Douglas and Kathleen Turner forming an acquaintance in *Romancing the Stone* (1984)

Troubles beset Michael Douglas as Jack Colton in *The Jewel of the Nile* (1985)

Michael Douglas's weekend fling turns into a horrendous nightmare in *Fatal Attraction* (1987)

Glenn Close meets Michael Douglas and wife, Anne Archer, in *Fatal Attraction* (1987)

Michael Douglas and Charlie Sheen living dangerously in *Wall Street* (1987)

Michael Douglas as the ruthless Gordon Gekko in *Wall Street* (1987)

Kathleen Turner, Danny De Vito and Michael Douglas in *War of the Roses* (1989)

Michael Douglas and Melanie Griffith as lovers in Nazi Germany in *Shining Through* (1991)

Sharon Stone and Michael Douglas sharing an intimate moment in *Basic Instinct* (1991)

Illustrations courtesy of Napthine–Walsh Collections.

Acknowledgements

This book would not have been possible without the assistance of a number of people. Annene Kaye and Jim Sclavunos produced an earlier book on Michael Douglas which was enormously informative. *Rolling Stone* magazine has featured Michael Douglas on several occasions and the standard of the research and writing opened many doors for me. The new breed of film magazines, notably *Empire* in the UK and *Première* in the States, have been immensely useful, particularly through the work of writers like Nancy Griffiths. To all of the writers who have wittingly or unwittingly assisted me in the production of this book my unstinting admiration and thanks.

On a personal level I should thank a number of people whose support sustains and encourages me. They are too many to list individually but the people who matter know who they are and how important they are to me.

1 Michael Douglas

There are countless strands which run through a life. Many become entwined and enmeshed making the tracing of motives and events immensely difficult. Emotions are one of the most abstruse elements of any life, and relationships between members of a family are among the most difficult aspects to understand objectively. The complexity of the relationship between a father and son is far-reaching, and the ramifications can have effects lasting through generations.

This is true for an ordinary working family, but the problems are exaggerated proportionately when the son is striving to strike up a relationship or establish his independence in the shadow of a famous father. Stories are legion of the difficulties faced by such individuals as Frank Sinatra Junior, Julian Lennon, and Gary Crosby. There are other lurid tales of wanton behaviour from the children of the famous, and psychological difficulties have made only the therapists happy, and rich.

Those undeniable family problems are made so

much worse when the famous father sires a son who develops a fame which equals his father's or even exceeds it. That is a rare phenomenon, particularly when both father and son excel in the same industry. In the entertainment business there are many stories of son trying to follow father, but there are very, very few of those tales which are happy. Who can forget the pain visibly suffered by Frank Sinatra Junior when his efforts at emulating his legendary dad faltered and then slipped away into failure?

Over the last fifteen years the Hollywood career of Kirk Douglas has been emulated and perhaps even slightly eclipsed by the dazzling success of his eldest son, Michael. A series of multi-million dollar income films like *Wall Street*, *Fatal Attraction*, and *Basic Instinct* have made Michael Douglas one of the most bankable stars in the world. So much so that, as Kirk Douglas has ruefully admitted on several occasions, these days he is known more for being the father of Michael Douglas than for being Kirk Douglas, three-times Oscar nominee.

The pressures of growing up in the shadow of a world-famous father clearly had their effects on Michael Douglas. He had the unpleasant experience of enduring adolescence and puberty in the full glare of a voracious tabloid press. Those difficult years are hard on any teenager, but very few have to suffer the indignities of seeing every spot and pimple displayed for the world to see.

The problems of puberty are exacerbated, often beyond tolerance, when suffered by children of the super-rich and super-accessible. There are those members of the film community – people like James Stewart and Henry Fonda – who are smiled upon by their peers, particularly the publicity machine. There are others – and Kirk Douglas is a prime example – who seemed to have set a deliberate course to offend and alienate the publicity moguls. That is the choice of such men as Kirk Douglas but unfortunately the effects are felt by younger, weaker members of his family. For many years Michael fitted into that category. Eventually he climbed beyond the point where the gossips and the journalists could hurt Kirk through him, and by that time he was too important to be deeply hurt by them either.

It is one of Michael's greatest achievements that he has managed to overcome his many personal problems as a youth to emerge triumphant as a successful businessman, a superstar, and an adult. He is recognized as a man's man, one of the few male film stars who can be admired and respected by men whilst simultaneously being an object of lust and desire for women. His cool, sardonic reaction to fame betrays his true feelings about his status and role, and it is also evident that he is a man who savours the lifestyle which his work and fame have brought him. Michael Douglas has matured greatly since those difficult days in the sixties.

Many other sons of famous fathers have not been so fortunte, consumed by ambitions and envies they often were unable to really understand. At times California seems populated by a strange breed of perpetual Peter Pans marooned in a never-never land fuelled by drugs, alcohol and every known excess. California is the traditional centre for the wilder side of life and the film community, and later the rock community, took full advantage of the possibilities.

It is undeniable that many people entertained doubts about the young Michael Douglas. During his hippie period in the sixties many informed commentators including his father were heard to doubt Michael's application, sense of values, and belief in the American Dream. During those tempestuous years there were many families rent by internal disputes, as the much-publicized generation gap took hold of western society. A number of successful films, most notably *The Graduate*, concentrated on the problems of family relationships and divisions, and alienation became a central theme. When he finally became an actor Michael's first few roles explored this question of division and alienation and for the second half of the sixties such themes dominated society and the arts.

In America it was the Vietnam War which crystallized the schisms between the young and their parents. The divisions cut across class, race and creed, and the battle lines were drawn simply

4

by age. Millions of families were split asunder by conflicts of opinion, and emotion, and it wasn't only the poor or even the middle classes who suffered.

Even the super-rich families like the dynasty founded by Kirk Douglas were not immune. Disputes between the young Michael and Kirk were many, and the father went out of his way to impress on Michael the fact that his choice of lifestyle was wrong.

It took some time, and a degree of heartache, before those doubting Thomases, and Kirks were forced to admit that Michael may not have been wrong after all. He was simply captivated then by a slightly different kind of American Dream. In the light of *Romancing the Stone* and its sequels, plus his rack of other massive successes, it is difficult to refute the argument that Michael Douglas was right all along.

And yet what personal strains must have been created between father and son as Michael lurched uncertainly from an unpromising period at school, to become a beatnik drop-out in California, and finally stumble uncertainly into an acting career. That film and television work was to elevate the son to world fame and bring accolades, like the Oscar for Best Actor in 1988, for which his father had hungered but never achieved.

For a man as compulsively ambitious and as totally career-orientated as Kirk Douglas the success of Michael must hve stimulated a violent mix of emotions. On the one hand a natural, instinctive pride at his son's accomplishments – on the other, darker hand is a maelstrom of meaner emotions prompted by professional pride and rivalry. Kirk Douglas, the generally admitted 'most unpopular man in Hollywood' and dutiful father, clearly loves his eldest son and is immensely proud of his achievements. At the same time Kirk Douglas, top gunslinger in town, is resentful of any challenge to his natural supremacy, even when, in commercial terms, it comes from his son.

The other sons have become successful in their own right, but none have approached Michael in terms of fame or earning power. When a brother, or half-brother, can be paid $14 million for a single film, or $350,000 for a car commercial voice-over it does push him on to a different plateau. His immense success has elevated Michael beyond his father and also way beyond his brother and half-brothers, and the strains imposed on the family structure must have been savage. Pride is there, but the personalities involved would not be human if there was not envy as well. The emotional energy expended in such sibling duels forced all the men into undeclared contests *à la* the Kennedys, to assert first their independence, then their superiority. Sadly, in the eyes of many, $14 million cheques tend to end any such contests as a serious exercise. To his brother and two half-brothers the success achieved by Michael Douglas must have had a slightly bitter aftertaste. After years spent living in the shadow of a famous father the boys were then forced to live with their own achievements overshadowed by those of an even more famous brother.

The Douglas clan has become rather reclusive over the years, and there are comparatively few pictures of father and all four sons together. Library collections reveal thousands of shots of Kirk, thousands more of Michael, and a multitude of Kirk and Michael together, but a scant handful of the entire dynasty. Peter and Eric the children of Kirk's second marriage are shadowy figures in comparison to their father and elder half-brother – a potentially difficult situation.

The adolescent rivalry shown by Michael to his father was played out on a world stage, and, because of the prurient interest of the Hollywood gossip columnists, all were made aware of it. The problems suffered by the other sons of Kirk Douglas were less publicized, partly because they were less public than him and partly because he was the eldest and first. Only Michael's difficulties became common knowledge.

And several controlled statements by Michael Douglas demonstrated how deeply he felt the ongoing situation. 'My father is obsessive – he watches himself all the time!' he remarked in one of his earliest interviews. Several years later he extended his views by declaring, 'What is hard to understand is the amount of public loving and praise a personality gets and measure that against some of the deprivation you feel. Here's the public saying, "You're wonderful, I love you, I want to kiss you", and you're the son or daughter sitting on the side.'

Kirk Douglas has spent a lifetime battling against prejudice and ill-treatment, real or imagined. His attitude has brought him the dislike, often hatred, of a number of people. A natural belligerence and assertiveness in the first half of his career gifted him with the title of 'Most Hated Man in Hollywood' awarded by *Photoplay* magazine. One of the less unpleasant descriptions of him came from Sheilah Graham who described Kirk as 'boastful, egotistical, and resentful of criticism – if anyone dare give it!' He lived up to this reputation and often seemed to delight in it but even in his more amenable moments he always seemed determined that nobody would ever put him into second place.

That attitude caused his almost legendary truculence and awkwardness. It also resulted in a situation where he would go to almost any lengths to be number one, as Ernest Borgnine ruefully recalled. 'In the film, *The Vikings*, every day I did a large number of action scenes and reaction shots. But something bothered me; the cameras always seemed a good way off, and Douglas somehow managed to find himself in close-up. When the film came out I was so far away I had difficulty recognizing myself. Alone Douglas's smile had the right to the close-ups.' It is not an exaggeration to state that Kirk Douglas caused fear in a wide range of his contemporaries.

With such a naturally competitive man it shouldn't be surprising if he reacted badly to any challenge to his supremacy from any quarter. Names from the great old days, people like John Wayne and Burt Lancaster and even the unfortunate Ernest Borgnine, were the early rivals, but there have been a steady stream ever since.

The young pretenders were always waiting in the wings, hoping for a slip from the old. It was Kirk's misfortune, and yet his delight, that one of those young gunslingers turned out to be his eldest son. He made many fervent declarations against Michael or any of his other sons going into the acting profession. As a result it must have been terribly galling – and exciting – to find his oldest son first defying his wishes and then becoming a hugely successful star.

The push to get his sons, particularly Michael, into safe, respectable professions like the law could not have been prompted by some instinctive fear of what they might achieve as actors. Rather it was an entirely natural wish to see his children spared the gnawing anxiety which is the actor's natural lot. 'Very few people, in general and in the movie business, criticize you constructively. They just want to destroy your confidence. I didn't want my boys to suffer that, and that's the reason,' admitted Kirk. 'I tried to discourage them from getting into pictures.'

Michael was the first son to receive the unsubtle nudges away from acting, but he was the only one to entirely discard the paternal advice. None of the other sons became actors but neither did they become lawyers or doctors as Kirk wished. Each of them became involved at some stage with the business but more on the technical or administrative side. Only Michael took that firm step in front of the cameras.

Once he defied his father's wishes and joined the acting profession Michael became an unwitting part of the powerful band of rivals to his father and he has since spent half a lifetime proving that Kirk really did have cause to worry. 'I was very conscious of my father's persona as an actor, his dynamic persona,' admitted Michael. 'And steering clear of anything that required anything near his kind of strength!'

However, it is indisputable that one of the traits which took Michael to the heights was that same power and strength.

2   The Lotus-eaters

California has been a schizophrenic state for almost the whole of the twentieth century. Every known vice and virtue and excess has been displayed, often wantonly, in the state since the days of the Californian Gold Rush and possibly before. But it is in its self-appointed role as one of the world's entertainment centres that the state's sybaritic nature has been most beautifully fulfilled.

Ever since film-makers looking for cheap facilities outside New York stumbled across a sleepy village named Hollywood the city of Los Angeles and the state of California have paraded a rich variety of personalities to the outside world.

Inevitably as the far western frontier it is the home of vast wealth and huge success; simultaneously there are the heart-rending tragedies often fuelled by that success or the loss of it. It is the western outpost of corporate America with multinational corporations entombed in their frosted glass citadels in Century City and downtown L.A.; there are also isolated artistic communities drawn by ghosts of the past and a symbiotic relationship with the mountains and the ocean and the edge of the nation.

The final frontier, the west coast – all the historical descriptions create the picture and mood of a lifestyle continually expanding and breaking the boundaries. New forms of technology emerged from California's Silicon Valley, and new ways of living in group harmony also appeared from the Golden State.

The various artistic communities have always been part of the history of California and, particularly, Hollywood. Perhaps surprisingly those working in the film industry have not been the only members of such communities. Writers, artists, designers, and free-thinkers of many kinds have been drawn to California to indulge in a lifestyle not readily available in less accommodating climates further east.

One manifestation of this lifestyle has been a variety of types of group living, often described as communes. The sprawling mass of the Hollywood Hills north of Ventura Boulevard has been home to a wild assortment of characters and communes, particularly during the sixties.

That period saw the establishment of an array of family-type groupings including dozens and often hundreds of people, all anxious to find an alternative lifestyle free from the crassly commercial concerns of middle America. Such lifestyles covered extremes of behaviour from the benign but bizarre like the Pranksters outside San Francisco to the evil and murderous like Charles Manson's Family in Hollywood.

Between those two extremes lay wide divergences in behaviour involving thousands of people. Some pleasant constants dominated most of the communes. The easy availability of sex, of drugs, of cheap food meant that the residents of the Californian communes enjoyed a hedonistic and sybaritic lifestyle of a type unrecognizable to most people on the planet.

Alfred Lord Tennyson wrote of 'The Lotus-eaters' in the nineteenth century describing the lifestyle of a race of people in ancient days. He would have been surprised, and perhaps delighted, to discover that the true Lotus-eaters were alive and well and living in southern California in the second half of the twentieth century.

Hundreds of different communes crystallized in the warm sunshine and the liberal, pre-Nixon climate. San Francisco became a focal point for the counter-culture with a generation taking root around the Haight-Ashbury intersection. Once the media began to focus on what was happening the people who were most sincere about an alternative lifestyle were already long gone, and many favoured a life out of California's towns and cities.

One of the more substantial communes was

13

found in Santa Barbara in a region known as Mountain Drive up in the hills to the north of the town. The hills known as the Californian Coastal Range sweep imperiously from the north of the state down to San Diego, guarding the coastline like a massive brooding, security fence.

There, in a rambling collection of neo-classical and Spanish-styled buildings, lived together almost one hundred and fifty people in a casual grouping. 'It wasn't formal,' remembers Cassie, one of the later arrivals, 'People just drifted in, stayed a while, then split. There were no hang-ups about possessiveness.'

Those 'lost souls' were joined in the mid sixties by Michael K. Douglas, ex-Choate and Beaverbrook pupil and drop-out from the University of California. He was also the son of a broken marriage although he had gained greatly from the stability of his mother's remarriage.

However, there were two distinctive features about the newcomer which separated him from all the other lotus-eaters. He was the only one to hold a plaque as 'Mobil Man of the Month', a salesmanship award from Mobil Oil. And he was the only one on the commune who was the son of a major film star, the 'most hated man in Hollywood', Kirk Douglas.

Like certain of the others on Mountain Drive he was a conspicuous failure, in varying degrees, at virtually everything he had ever undertaken. His peers in the commune covered all spectrums of

American society. 'A lot of them were older people in their thirties and forties who had once held white-collar jobs, and who had dropped out in the days of the beatniks,' remembered Michael.

Dropping out had become more prevalent during the late fifties during the so-called beatnik period, but as the sixties arrived the flood became an epidemic. Guru of the Alternative Society, Timothy Leary, exhorted 'Turn On, Tune In, Drop Out!' and thousands of men and women, including those drifting along on Mountain Drive, took his lead.

Many of them had been conspicuous successes in the earlier part of their lives. Many were members of comfortable middle-class professions and they, ex-accountants and lawyers and teachers, had taken a conscious decision to abandon Californian materialism to live alongside Michael Douglas in the hills. The lifestyle was highly idiosyncratic. 'We worked on the basis of enough,' remembered Cassie. 'As long as there was enough of what everyone needed, then nobody had worries. Nobody had hang-ups.'

This kind of idealistic sharing was solid, but relatively short-lived. While it survived it meant that possessions played comparatively little part in the lives of the members of the commune. Michael had a room with a bed, and a few clothes, and very little else. For that period it didn't seem to matter. 'Nobody had anything much, but we shared what we had. And for a time it was beautiful, really beautiful.'

'I lived above the kitchen,' remembered Michael Douglas fondly. 'We were the only ones in the neighbourhood who had a swimming-pool. So it was all nude, everybody was just nude. I remember once we got arrested for indecent exposure.'

The staples of life were what mattered in that environment, but they were staples markedly different from those recognized in more conventional circles. 'It was sex and drugs, that's all. Grass and tabs of acid and getting laid. I can't remember anything more important than that. Sure we must have eaten – nobody starved – but it just didn't seem such a big deal!' recalled another commune dweller.

The casual sex was an obvious delight for a healthy 20-year-old man, especially one who had been relatively limited in his contact with women previously. 'He wasn't a monk before he went to Mountain Drive,' another commune-dweller admitted. 'But he suddenly discovered that women were attracted to him, and no guy is going to waste an opportunity like that!'

His mother had first become aware of his attraction for the opposite sex while he was at school. She took a call from his counsellor who told her that Michael was 'like catnip to the young ladies'. The report went on to complain that his work had become progressively worse, and that he was receiving a steady stream of notes in class from girls. Shortly after this conversation he was removed from that school and sent to Eaglebrook prep school.

An almost legendary capacity for female company was allegedly one of Kirk's problems. Michael's unashamed love of women was first seen and developed in the commune. It was to remain with him, occasionally surfacing in exciting bursts of sexual activity such as during the wild promotional tour for *One Flew Over the Cuckoo's Nest* with Jack Nicholson.

The shy boy, nervous and uncertain of women, was brought rapidly to sexual maturity by the easy liaisons within the commune. Of course in that less traumatic time the dangers of casual, unprotected sex had not emerged as the killer plague now seen ravaging society. It was possible for girls like Cassie to drop into a sexual relationship lasting as little as a few hours without giving any thought to implications of danger.

The lifestyle in the balmy sunshine of California could not have been more carefree. No responsibilities, no duties, no need for concerns other than satisfying desires and exploring thoughts normally frowned on by more mundane or conventional areas of society.

The sweetness of the life was increased by the frequent, perhaps compulsive use, of various drugs. Just as with sex the attraction of the drugs was in their sheer ease of availability. To a community like that on Mountain Drive drugs were an essential part of everyday life. Blowing grass or dropping a tab of acid was as commonplace as eating or sleeping, but as drugs were essential to the maintenance of the communal lifestyle they assumed an importance even greater than food or sleep.

Benzedrine, phenmetrazine, methedrine, quaaludes plus a whole cocktail of other substances like peyote, mescaline and magic mushrooms were generally available, but it was grass and LSD which became the normal drug diet not only of the commune-dwellers but of a whole generation. By the time the commune embraced Michael Douglas the residents were able to obtain regular, cheap supplies of high-grade marijuana like Acapulco Gold and also the ubiquitous Lyserg-Saure-Diathylamid, better known as LSD.

This mysterious substance had been part of the scientific world since the late thirties when it became an element in research into circulatory aids. A chemist, Albert Hoffman, working for a Swiss-based pharmaceutical company named Sandoz, was engaged in investigations into the medicinal potential of lysergic acid. Several years' work in this field had failed to produce positive results and the research was suspended in 1938. Hoffman continued to work in private on his last formula, LSD-25, and on 16 April 1943 Hoffman was the first unwitting victim of an LSD trip.

Some years later the CIA began investigating possible uses for LSD in terms of its mind-altering properties and thus began a shameful period in which volunteers and even patients in mental hospitals were given the drug to test its effects. LSD was promoted by a number of luminaries including Leary and Ken Kesey, but the true High Priest of the movement in California was Owsley.

Augustus Owsley Stanley, 111, became irretrievably connected with the drug, and indeed was once described in an FBI memorandum as 'the man who did for LSD what Henry Ford did for the motor car'.

He earned a sizeable fortune from LSD but was intent on spreading the gospel as he saw it and so he simply gave away massive quantities of the drug. A study in late 1965 revealed that almost four million Americans had tried LSD, with some seventy per cent being high school or college students. Because of the Summer of Love and Vietnam and other elements that number of experimenters rose markedly higher during the next few years.

Owsley had almost single-handedly been responsible for the spreading of the drug in California, even though the Federal Government had moved against the drug in February 1965. A law was passed outlawing the manufacture of LSD but it was three years later that the federal law was amended to make possession illegal. This change came in the wake of several states' legislatures deciding to make possession a criminal offence. California had acted against possession of LSD in 1966 but it made little practical difference.

The great San Franciscan Be-Ins of 1966 and 1967 and even the Monterey Festival took place after California had made possession illegal, and these events, among many others, were virtually fuelled by LSD. The drug was freely available to those who wanted it, and communities like Mountain Drive encountered no difficulty in gathering supplies of chemical stimulants. 'We smoked a lot of pot and dropped a lot of LSD. I took quite a lot of both. I liked it!' commented Douglas.

The commune even tried a little agrarian self-help and feverish attempts took place to grow top quality grass in the brittle soil high above Santa Barbara. There among the honeysuckle and the wild bougainvillaea grew a variety of pot plants cultivated by inhabitants of the commune.

Michael didn't have any agricultural leanings. He smoked the pot, in copious quantities, but never displayed any interest in producing the substance. Not that it mattered. 'We were all pot-heads!' recalled another resident. 'There was so much of the stuff coming through every day, and then some girl started growing it up back behind the big house. We ended up with a garden of grass. Really!'

The struggle became one not of survival but one of easing the way through the day, of staving off the possibility of boredom. In most instances that didn't happen. The group, or rather small splinters of the total assemblage, would wander off to spend the long Californian day lazing around talking and laughing, skinny-dipping in pools, or presenting their own version of amateur theatre.

Perhaps it was there, in these artlessly contrived mini-plays, that his later acting inclinations first surfaced, but anything approaching a job or a career was anathema at that time to Michael and his fellow lotus-eaters. Most of them had worked, at various times and in various callings, but there had been a general cutting of ties with the commercial world. Careers and work simply didn't matter.

Not so for his father. Kirk was a massive star in Hollywood throughout the sixties, and living less than forty miles from the commune Michael became a constant source of embarrassment and irritation to him and the family. Many people within the Hollywood community were aware that Michael had been taken to Norway to work among the general crew on *The Heroes of Telemark* and then Israel to work on *Cast a Giant Shadow*.

It is not surprising that many eyebrows were raised at Michael's sudden decision to abandon Hollywood, and work, and the more acceptable lifestyles readily available to him in Beverly Hills. Gossip columnists, who still retained semblances of their old, awesome power, exacerbated the situation, and the fierce pride of Kirk Douglas was very severely tested by Michael's apparent wantonness. The scandal caused by the discovery that the eldest son of Kirk Douglas was living in a hippie colony is hard to comprehend now, but it generated enormous adverse publicity at the time.

An uncomfortable example of double standards became evident. Hollywood morality could hardly be held up as an example and hadn't been since before the distant days of Fatty Arbuckle and Charlie Chaplin. In comparison with some of his father's well-documented exploits Michael's sojourn in the commune was almost domesticated, but there was one major difference. What he was doing was not the norm, and Hollywood has always demanded observance of the status quo.

He was bucking the system, displaying visible contempt for the straights in Los Angeles, and such arrogance attracted more than its fair share of vitriol. Inevitably much of the abuse and the sarcasm directed at hippie Michael was a thinly veiled attack on his father. The huge number of enemies created by Kirk Douglas during his career meant that a chance to extract a little revenge, even at the expense of his son, was too good to miss.

The lifestyle enjoyed by those in the commune contrasted violently with Kirk's stern, puritanical devotion to work. His terse refusal to comment on the commune lifestyle gives an indication of the strength of his feelings on the lifestyle adopted by his eldest son. He couldn't ignore or even forget the existence of the commune. His many enemies in the press took lurid delight in regaling tales, often wildly exaggerated, of what Kirk's son was really doing. Some of the stories about the communes which appeared in the more sensational American publications are scarcely credible. They were brutal fabrications, nothing else.

Kirk only made one visit to the commune during Michael's sojourn, and that did not result in any fruitful exchange of views. Kirk was clearly unhappy – a contemporary claims 'appalled!' – by the living conditions and the sheer attitude of *laissez-faire* which was the operating rule at Mountain Drive. He visited his son once but never came back. As one of the columnists commented at the time, 'If the kid had been in San Quentin he'd have had more visits!'

But it shouldn't be thought that the young Michael Douglas was distressed by his father's evident disapproval. The very fact of moving into the commune was a gesture of rebellion, of rejection of various aspects of his father's life. The visible dislike of the commune lifestyle constantly displayed by his father was, in a strange way, confirmation to Michael that he had made the right choice. As he ruefully commented several years later, 'My old man wasn't just Kirk Douglas but this enormous being, this dynamic, magnetic presence. Damned if he wasn't Spartacus himself.

I never felt I could measure up to my dad or be anything like him, so I quit trying. I dropped out, stopped competing and became the opposite of everything he was.'

That element of competition underpinned many of the personal problems which beset the relationship between father and son in the late sixties. Many American families were ripped apart by similar tensions, and the youth revolt caused a series of alienations which took years to heal.

Politically the young often differ violently from their parents and Michael's uncompromisingly liberal stance over issues dominant in the sixties, particularly Vietnam, was not calculated to endear himself to his father. Although Kirk's views were far more mainstream than those of contemporaries like John Wayne he was still a long way to the right of Michael.

The eldest Douglas son was an intelligent, perceptive young man who would not soften his views for anyone. He freely expressed his opinions to anybody who would listen but expressions like 'All I really ask for is a free national election in Vietnam. I'm sure the Communists would win!' infuriated many.

He even found time to express his strong opinions on Vietnam in terms of his father's profession, another barb whose target could not have been unintentional. 'I'm totally against the war. And for that reason I'm very happy that these big studios . . . these big industries . . . are making pictures against the war. That shows how prevalent anti-war feelings must be now.'

His period as a commune-dweller coincided with the emergence of all the ghosts which came to haunt America during those tempestuous times in the middle sixties. Such dreadful events as the twin assassinations of Dr Martin Luther King and Bobby Kennedy, the slaying of Malcolm X, the race riots in Watts and elsewhere, the brutal suppression of youthful protest in Chicago at the Democratic Convention, and above all the dreadful spectre of Vietnam.

These nightmares were enough to drive many thousands of people out of the country. A large number of young men, anxious to avoid the draft, left for Canada or Scandinavia or Europe. Other, older people, sickened by what they perceived as a growing bestiality in their homeland, departed for other shores. Still more, like Michael Douglas, stayed bodily in America but encouraged their minds to voyage elsewhere.

The commune was a mystical retreat where he could undergo his 'rites of passage' and prepare for manhood. And if that initiation involved mind-expandiing drugs and orgiastic sex who was to say he was wrong? Given the evident craziness outside the safe haven of Mountain Drive it might be considered that Michael Douglas had, for that specific period, made entirely the right and sensible choice.

The commune wasn't a commitment for life. It couldn't be. Even characters like Cassie would slip away as times changed and the easy familiarity of the sixties was strangled by the coldness of the new decade. The chilling end of the sixties and his growing maturity ensured that Michael would eventually abandon the commune, and slowly, sheepishly return to the real world. But it would not be a speedy or even a painless transition.

'I saw that most of those people just weren't very happy. Oh, it was pleasant enough sitting naked by a pool cramming drugs down your throat!' admitted Douglas. 'It felt good . . . like a total sensual experience. But you weren't doing anything. It was like retiring at 21!'

As the years rolled by Michael would become sometimes reticent and sometimes nostalgic about the commune period and about the delicate idealism which fuelled his thoughts and behaviour at that time. Only occasional remarks betray the warmth of his memories of the life on Mountain Drive, but it is obvious that the character of the man who emerged as a film superstar was moulded in that exclusive community. A personality developed as a result of the experiences and mental expansions prompted by the commune, and there is more than a residue of Michael Douglas, the hippie, in the modern Michael Douglas, film star, super businessman and Oscar winner.

3 An Actor's Life

Possibly the hardest single change Michael Douglas ever had to make was the one from hippie to actor. Perhaps this was occasioned by a growing disillusionment with the commune lifestyle; it must also be admitted that the heady idealism of the early and middle sixties died on the vine as the end of the decade approached. Equally likely is the possibility that the change was induced by a growing maturity and desire to find some goal in life. In this respect the importance of the Douglas genes cannot be underestimated. The role model presented by his father, Kirk, had instilled an abiding knowledge of the business in Michael and his brothers.

When he eventually returned to college after his extended sabbatical he was compelled to declare a subject and, without any forward planning, elected for English. During his final two years at college he slipped unobtrusively into acting, thanks to the doors which his English course opened for him. 'I joined the drama club and decided I loved acting!'

The early organized forays into acting came via theatre work, made slightly unpalatable by a massive dose of stage fright. This was a problem which would afflict him greatly during his first steps in the profession and make many of his early performances notable only for the regularity and volume of his vomiting. Those initial acting experiences brought him his first awards, being voted 'Best Actor of the Year' and then receiving the 'Director of the Year' award from the University of California in 1968.

And those early experiences gave him a love of theatre work which has never left him. Many years later he would seriously consider returning to the New York stage but a massive financial offer from the film world diverted him once again. It is doubtful now that circumstances could conspire to pull him back to the stage, but it remains his favourite medium.

The initial reactions of his father did not assist Michael to be convinced that he had made the right choice. Rather over-strenuous criticism of stage performances were doubtless made for the best reasons with Kirk still harbouring ambitions for Michael in a safe, respectable profession like medicine or the law.

However, even well-intentioned criticism can wound and Kirk's reported words caused scars which were not easily healed. Not for the first time the media were not slow to see the potential for gossip and scandal in the Douglas father-son relationship. Having covered the hippie commune period, and voraciously examined the conflict between Michael and Kirk, the American press was quick to seize on the new area of conflict. Kirk's thoughts on Michael's early Shakespearean appearances were extensively quoted, and the press gleefully awaited Michael's fiery reaction.

None was forthcoming. Instead he carried on cultivating his chosen craft via a number of unusual routes.

One of the most bizarre was guerilla or confrontational theatre. 'This was very much part of the times,' remembered Tim Planovitch, a veteran of off-Broadway productions. 'We would force our way into classes and stage a short performance. This would be a faked stabbing or a shooting. The kids and the teachers wouldn't know what was happening, and usually we'd cause some panic. During that panic we'd get into a speech about what was going down in Vietnam. In those days everything revolved around 'nam and the war.'

The Asian conflict had reverberations throughout the United States, but particularly on the college generation. Michael Douglas was firmly in that bracket, and was clearly at risk of conscription and a harrowing, possibly fatal, trip to Vietnam. Fortunately the discovery of a brace of displaced vertebrae meant that the Board classified him as I-Y. In the arcane workings of the American Conscription Board such a grade meant that the holder was considered unfit for military service. Being I-Y Michael Douglas was exempt from the draft, and was spared the horrors of Vietnam.

With a college record and a damning medical report as a result of his back problems, Michael could honourably avoid Vietnam. Many thousands of other young men missed the draft because of problems or 'disabilities' less serious than displaced vertebrae, and Michael, like them, was able to continue his life in the States. And he has not been completely free from back-related problems during the years since Vietnam.

His back problems were exaggerated, but who could legitimately blame Michael, or Kirk, for that? Any young man would obviously seek to avoid being dispatched to the hell-hole which was Vietnam. Any parent would take advantage of any loophole to lift a son out of the draft.

Michael Douglas missed direct immersion in Vietnam but the progress and conduct of the war had a major effect on his personality. Like so many members of his generation he found that his developing years were dominated and blighted by the war, and so many of his activities revolved around Vietnam.

He worked very successfully in an anti-war play called *Summertree* written by a friend, Ron Cowan. The play appeared during a happy period spent in Waterford, Connecticut at the Eugene O'Neill Theatre Centre, where he spent several summers. The Centre was a complex based on a superior mansion plus a barn, and a large garden leading down to a rugged beach on Long Island South. Into this creative nirvana poured authors and players from across the country for viewings, workshops and a general exposure to drama.

At that time the acting skills of the young Michael Douglas were not sufficiently developed for him to obtain major roles in the workshop productions. Instead he secured a minor role in return for muscle power expended in the construction of an amphitheatre constructed to the Greek model close by the barn.

Graduation, and a degree, allowed him to leave California and head back to New York for some serious work. The American Place Theatre deep in the village was his first working home, and there he came together with the legendary Wynn Handman. Having established a professional base he began to look seriously for work and met an unexpected problem – his name.

The various American television and stage unions had a long-standing registration for a man named Michael Douglas. Fortunately this restriction did not also apply to the film unions otherwise his later film career could well have been affected. Naturally the first Mr Douglas was not willing to change his name and so it fell to Kirk's son to make the first move. The younger

Mr Douglas had to adopt a slightly changed name in order to get work in those fields, and so some of his early appearances came under the imposing name of Michael K. Douglas.

'This name game has been a pain. I have to be M.K. Douglas on stage and in television because there's a Michael Douglas in Boston who has already registered with Actors' Equity and AFTRA. But I can be Michael Douglas in the movies because there is no-one by that name in the Screen Actors' Guild.'

He was also able to develop a network of friends and colleagues in New York which would stand him in good stead in his later climb to superstardom. People like John Guare, Michael Lessac and Danny De Vito became firm friends, and those friendships have lasted a quarter of a century. 'The best thing about being in New York was that I made a lot of good friends. And it was the first time I found myself really accomplishing something. In college I was just irresponsible. So I gained a lot of self-esteem working in New York. And I had three close friends, and we're all still friends. I remember it as continuing that communal spirit of '67.'

Danny De Vito has since worked successfully with Michael Douglas on several of his film projects including *One Flew Over the Cuckoo's Nest*, *Romancing the Stone*, *Jewel of the Nile* and *War of the Roses*.

On first sight there is little to connect the

handsome, rugged leading man with the squat, ugly De Vito. They obviously come from different worlds but there is a close bond which was created during the years of struggle and deprivation in New York. There is also a career similarity in that both of them came through to film stardom after major success in a long-running television series. For Douglas it was *Streets of San Francisco*; for De Vito it was the sly, selfish controller in *Taxi*.

'De Veets is one of my oldest buddies. 1967 was the first year we both got paid as actors – $65 a week – it's a big moment in your life – when we were room-mates in New York,' remembered Douglas fondly.

Work started to come through for him and Douglas achieved a breakthrough in February 1969 with his television debut in a long drama, *The Experiment*, which was part of the CBS Playhouse series. In keeping with the sentiments of the times the television play told the story of two rebels fighting to keep their individuality and self-respect in the face of the corporate system.

Michael Douglas played a hippie scientist caught in an ideological and moral struggle against the establishment. He was highly praised for his performance as Wilson Evans. He played this intense type of role so often that he clearly had a great deal of sympathy and affinity with the feelings and sentiments of men like Evans. The work brought him his first taste of public adulation and also the first of a stream of flattering comparisons with Kirk. New York commuters on the morning after the broadcast could read columnist Jack Gould who reported that 'the younger Mr Douglas could easily go as far as his father'.

This became a standard preface to any review or comment. It would be several years before his work would be described or criticized in its own right and not as part of a wider canon involving his father's many performances.

Michael Douglas was stunned by the reaction. 'It was amazing. I was doing a play, off-Broadway, and when I was riding to work that day on the subway people kept coming up to me and saying, "I saw you last night"!'

Fortunately all those initial comparisons between film star father and TV/theatre star son were very complimentary. Most pundits then thought he seemed set for a successful television career, although later events make it clear that Michael's long-term ambitions always lay in films, even though he did achieve that successful television career.

And then came that first feature film, *Hail Hero!*, John Weston's anti-war diatribe, which provided his first starring role less than a year after graduating from the University of California. When the announcement was made that Michael had secured his first starring part Kirk was in convalescence after a minor operation on nodes in the throat. Whether he was thrilled or terrified is not recorded. He wasn't able to speak. Reportedly he expressed his sentiments by grabbing a pad and etching the immortal message, 'I'm speechless!'

The part of yet another angry young man misunderstood by his stern father seemed to be made for Michael Douglas. For a period he seemed in danger of becoming typecast as the sixties' angry young man. It was a pity that he had to make his debut in such a shabby, amateurish piece which was based on thin arguments and empty rhetoric.

After *Hail Hero!* the reviewers once more concentrated on the parallels between the film's father-son relationship and that between the film's star and his own father.

Michael's work was not criticized unduly but the film itself was never going to pull up any saplings let alone Sequoias. He is careful never to criticize his early work but of *Hail, Hero!* he did ruefully comment, 'Maybe I was slightly exploited!'

The cast was hardly the most indistinguished with which Michael Douglas has ever been associated. The considerable talents of Arthur Kennedy also appeared in *Hail, Hero!* and the feature players included a very young Peter Strauss. And director, David Miller, had already distinguished himself as a brave and inventive director. He had even established an important link with the Douglas family being the director of the film which many, including Kirk himself, consider to be his finest ever film, *Lonely Are The Brave*.

Most of Michael's early films, pieces like *Hail Hero!*, *Napoleon and Samantha* and *Summertree* have not survived even in the modern form of video. Some who have managed to see all of them are not surprised. Douglas is philosophical about the situation. 'I was good, the movies didn't work out. So you're perceived as having had your shot.'

That first film also substantiated a long-standing link between Michael Douglas and the director, David Miller. Back when Miller directed *Lonely are the Brave* the editing room had provided the pubescent Michael Douglas with his first tentative experience in the nuts and bolts of the industry. It is difficult to conceive how such work performed by the son of the star of the film could remain unnoticed by the director. However, Michael Douglas was and is adamant that his family relationship played no part in his securing the starring role in the film. He insisted, however implausibly, that 'Miller didn't even know me when I walked in to test for the part.'

Such unlikely admissions whetted the appetites of the media hacks and for a period Michael became a prominent provider of interview material. His first taste of real success and fame made Michael an even more attractive target for media attention.

The fact that he had secured a leading part in a television play and a starring role in a film within his first year in the business marked him out as someone worthy of notice.

His notable family connections only added to that lustre, as he was quick and ready to admit. 'Being Kirk Douglas's son can't hurt an acting career . . . it can't make you a star either.' His cheerfully unguarded speech made him an irresistible magnet for the hacks and the gossip writers.

For a period Michael Douglas talked. On virtually any topic, and for virtually any interviewer, and it seemed that he only required a tape recorder and a running tape to provide wonderful material for the hacks.

Many of his public pronouncements were foolish and unwise, and would return to haunt him in future years. Remarks on politics and religion were particularly forthright, and the only subject on which he seemed able to be discreet was his relationship with his father. Despite incessant taunts and pleas he was usually able to steer conversations away from Kirk and on to more general, though hardly less controversial, topics. That unlikely discretion has remained with him and developed into a polished, almost political skill.

Several interviewers were intent only on trying to explore the soft scarred flesh of the father-son relationship.

He milked the publicity, and the hacks milked him, but it would be many years before he could free himself of the indiscretions committed during that early period.

A more serious career blunder came in his decision to turn down a role in one of the biggest film successes of the seventies. Michael York, John Voight, Beau Bridges, and Michael Sarrazin had earlier turned down the role as a male lead in *Love Story*. Michael Douglas rejected the part and thereby also passed on the opportunity to utter the immortal line, 'Love means never having to say you're sorry!'

More important was the fact that he missed the chance to benefit from the success of the film. Much of Ryan O'Neill's career was founded solely on his simpering appearance in *Love Story*. At the time Michael Douglas would have been grateful for such early success. 'It was a struggle for him to find something in which he wouldn't automatically be compared with Kirk,' remembered a family friend.

However, the fact that he would even be considered for the leading role in a big budget Paramount production was recognition of his growing stature within the industry. Erich Segal's book had achieved mass popularity and the subsequent film was freely expected to be a big hit. Nobody could have anticipated its immense impact.

His second film project, *Adam at 6 a.m.*, took

him away to Missouri for location shooting. The film detailed the exploits of a college professor who leaves his comfortable existence in California to work as a labourer in the Midwest for the summer vacation. It is a routine rites of passage tale, meant to examine complex issues of role-playing and the changing role of men in society. It became a series of arrows most of which were well-aimed but fell wide of their target.

Shooting in Orrick, Missouri, proved an engrossing experience, but it also proved an important guide for the future. This was his first prolonged spell in the heart of America, away from the disparate lures of the west and east coasts. The weeks in Orrick gave him an insight into a world of which he had read but had very little experience.

Those long dusty weeks in Missouri enabled him to study the mechanics of film production in a detail which clearly stimulated and excited him. His later award-winning work in producing films like *One Flew Over the Cuckoo's Nest* and *Romancing the Stone* may not have been born in Orrick, Missouri but it certainly received a massive boost there. His later dedication to the small points, to caring for the comforts of cast and crew, received an important grounding in Missouri where a giant, specially designed, bus was provided for the crew and equipment.

The abilities he brought to the role as producer

were founded on a basic appreciation of the importance of taking care of all those working on a film. In terms of film history *Adam at 6 a.m.* is notable for little other than enabling Michael Douglas to learn about the multi-faceted world of producing. 'He always said later that *Streets of San Francisco* was his college period for producing,' stated Ron Brown, film and television critic. 'But *Adam at 6 a.m.* was definitely his school period. Useless as a film, but a great learning ground for Douglas.'

The film was not a commercial success, but Michael's contribution received limited critical praise. More recognized was the performance of a young Joe Don Baker although co-producer Rick Rosenberg felt that Michael 'has so much more authority. He has grown so much'.

Many reviewers at the time were less aware of his growth and unaware of his new-found authority. Few papers were ready to praise the film and among the few complimentary remarks were George Patursky's, 'This intelligent drama, *Adam at 6 a.m.* presents a powerful dramatic dilemma deep in the Midwest where two young new talents shine. The screenplay, from local writers Elinor and Howard Karpf, very accurately conveys a taste of the sheer scale of the area.'

Despite the occasional review which praised the film there were far more which dismissed it. *Adam at 6 a.m.* vanished quietly and with little evidence of general regret. Even those involved in the film found it difficult in later years to boast their involvement. By his general reticence on the film Michael Douglas seemed to echo that faint embarrassment or distaste. At the time he couldn't afford the luxury of lengthy analysis of his work. It was more important to find another job.

On this occasion there was no desperation to seek out or wait for another project. Kirk's earlier purchase of the rights to Ron Cowan's *Summertree* had finally reached fruition. With a wicked echo of Woody Allen's laments about his Jewish mother Michael commented, 'My father, in his good Jewish mind, decided to do something for his son, put him in a movie.' Fortunately for Michael's long-term career, and peace of mind, Kirk wasn't arranging Michael's breakthrough into the business. By the time *Summertree* became a viable film project Michael had already completed two films. Neither of them had become huge hits but they were entirely Michael's; nobody could point at either film, wink knowingly, and whisper conspiratorially about Kirk opening doors.

The resulting film became a plodding, dreary venture. As an exercise in film technique it provided ample evidence of the supreme diffi- culty of turning an exciting play into even a passable film. *Summertree* had few virtues, and Michael Douglas wasn't one of them.

It was another piece so typical of its time. So

much of the drama, cinema, and music of that period had a common link. The brutalities of Vietnam dominated the soul of America for the second half of the sixties and inevitably that experience seared its way across the artistic community. Writers and artists struggled to produce works reflecting their horror at the war, and that dark period in America's history was gloomily reflected in the various creative out-pourings.

Summertree presented a miasma of personal ambiguities played out against the uncompromising background of the Vietnam War. Michael Douglas played yet another desperately earnest young man, but his acting credentials were set against a mature and accomplished supporting cast including Jack Warden and Barbara Bel Geddes, showing as yet no trace of her *Dallas* experiences.

Also in the cast was a young, darkly beautiful, actress named Brenda Vaccaro who had enjoyed a much more eventful career than Michael. She had already worked in many areas of the business from modelling through to Broadway, and she had even appeared prominently in an Oscar-winning film. Some five years older than Michael, she had featured in *Midnight Cowboy* with Dustin Hoffman and John Voight in 1969, some considerable time before *Summertree*.

Brenda Vaccaro and Michael Douglas were to become, in the coy prose of the gossip columns, 'an item'. When they decided to start living together it caused something of a prurient stir whipped up by the hypocritical baiting of the press.

Not for the first time Michael's public lifestyle caused a certain amount of controversy. To his credit he refused to disguise or distort his activities. He has never run away from problems, and while his candour has often dropped him into further problems he has been unusually open in matters about his private life. This contrasts vividly with the discretion, or should it be deceit, shown by so many other Hollywood luminaries.

His life might have been somewhat easier if he had decided to keep more information private but his frankness in those years came as something of a relief after the careful lies of so many contemporaries. Kirk also made several statements giving his blessing to the unofficial union.

As had happened some years earlier in the case of his commune lifestyle his public candour astonished many, not least those other Hollywood stars living similarly non-married lives but maintaining a more acceptable public face. Dozens of stars had enjoyed the benefits of the free love ethos, but Michael Douglas was unusually open in discussing such pleasures. Many personalities took drugs, but Michael Douglas was one of the few to freely admit it. Most personalities had mistresses, or marriages which were a complete sham; Michael Douglas was bold enough to defy convention by stating that he was living with a woman without the safety net of the marriage certificate.

Brenda and Michael settled together as a pair, and the arrangement seemed to suit them both. 'She doesn't feel any need to get married, and I share that view completely,' admitted Michael. 'In the old days a woman was trapped in the cliché of "getting her man". Today she doesn't have to feel that way and her life, hopefully, becomes richer and fuller. She didn't have the immediate necessity of getting married hanging over her head. There are other things in her life.'

Once again the papers and magazines homed in on Kirk's alleged displeasure with Michael. The father went out of his way to express upbeat sentiments about the non-conventional choice made by Michael, declaring a hitherto unsuspected belief in couples living together and a touching faith in the new couple. 'Michael has gotten less promiscuous . . . he's been with a lot of different girls, but he's settled down with Brenda. I think she's terrific.'

Brenda Vaccaro became a major part of Michael's life, and they settled, perhaps surprisingly, to a routine of quiet domesticity. For a lengthy period they seemed content to be just an ordinary couple spending time on east and west coasts and, perhaps most enjoyably, in the lushness of Vermont. It didn't suit the gossip columnists to find Michael Douglas living the life of quiet tranquillity with a single woman. He was baited yet again by some of the more scurrilous publications but the couple were, for a period at least, beyond such pettiness. They were more concerned with building a life together which would allow the personal freedom to grow and develop as artists while remaining together.

It must be recognized that Michael Douglas had never enjoyed the kind of ordinary domestic life which most people take completely for granted. As a child he had been one of the tiny victims of the bitter divorce of his parents. His teenage years were spent in constant bewildering transit between two utterly different worlds, on west and east coasts. Periods at boarding school, then college, were followed by the time spent in the distended artificiality of the commune. Beyond that lay the long months trying to get work in New York, and for virtually the whole of these different periods he lived a lifestyle entirely separate from the domesticity which became the norm with Brenda. For a variety of reasons he eagerly grasped the quiet life which was what both of them wanted at that time in their lives. It didn't escape the notice of the media machine that Kirk's son, the rebel, had become Joe Normal, and Michael was subject to some merciless sarcasm in the press.

Careers were not forgotten or neglected, and both sought the kind of work to provide a professional challenge and also to advance their flourishing reputations. Michael achieved both aims in his portrayal of Jerry the Naz in *Pinkville*, an important off-Broadway production in the early seventies.

The play ran in the round for six weeks at the American Palace Theatre. Once again it allowed Michael to exorcize his Vietnam ghosts through drama. By that time he had made a series of controversial statements on Vietnam and had become something of an outspoken critic of Lyndon Johnson and the various warlords in the American military machine.

He played the unlikely role of a new marine arriving at training camp with a strong aversion to killing. The resultant emotional conflicts are exacerbated by a sadistic sergeant who goads and manipulates the sensitive recruit with a terrible result. At the end of the training period the formerly passive and gentle recruit leaves for Vietnam as a programmed killing machine.

Set in the round the play achieved a powerful intimacy which appealed to Michael Douglas. 'I like it that way. It's more intimate, but it also requires great concentration,' he stated. 'You can hear every little noise.'

Sometimes incongruously the play used music at various points to complement or support the plotline. Michael Douglas was called upon to sing and apparently made a fair job of it. 'He was no Pavarotti but he had a nice, light tenor voice. He wouldn't have made a career in musicals, but he wasn't disgraced by any means,' remembered Anne Buchanan, who saw several of the performances.

It must have helped that the staging of the play coincided with the trial of Lieutenant Calley, the hapless U.S. Marine responsible for the My Lai massacre. The intense media coverage of the trial, and the grim revelations about what supposedly civilized Americans could do, make the theme of *Pinkville* very relevant to many people and to the time. In reflection on My Lai and *Pinkville* Michael Douglas commented, 'The blame lies in the philosophy of the training, where one gets his attitude.'

Not for the last time in his career Douglas appeared in a piece reflecting a major public concern of the moment and a piece which received copious amounts of publicity because of the general problem it was coincidentally reflecting.

The play achieved a notoriety in New York theatrical circles which made it one of the successes of that season. Off-Broadway productions had traditionally been able to deal with meatier material than the more entertainment orientated Great White Way. Controversial topics like the story of Jerry the Naz found a home off-Broadway which was denied elsewhere. Patrons visited such theatres expecting thought-provoking, disturbing drama, and *Pinkville* certainly didn't disappoint.

Its impressive success was formally recognized when Michael won the Theatre World Award. Coincidentally Brenda had won the same award some ten years earlier.

Michael's work was developing across a broad spectrum. His award-winning performances off-Broadway was added to starring roles in films, and a developing career in television. The various networks had a voracious appetite for scripts, and actors and actresses, and Michael Douglas was in regular demand for television work.

One such appearance was to have a major impact on his future life and career. He had worked for a number of producers and directors with varying degrees of success, but he performed on several occasions for a producer who was already in the process of building an empire.

Quinn Martin's name appeared on a huge number of programmes in the sixties and seventies. He developed a speciality in quick turn-over police and detective stories, and it was one of his innumerable American series, *FBI*, which produced the situation which gave Michael Douglas his first significant exposure.

He filmed several episodes of a variety of programmes for Quinn Martin including one episode of *FBI*. This otherwise unmemorable performance certainly took the eye of the producer as Michael inadvertently acted out one whole scene with his fly wide open.

Those initial contacts with Quinn Martin

allowed Michael's agent to suggest his name for a new Quinn Martin cops 'n robbers production to be called *Streets of San Francisco*. Despite the recommendation from his agents Michael was instinctively against the idea, mainly because he still carried a residue of the old resentment against television. The snobbery in acting dictated that theatre work was acceptable, even desirable, with film work an acceptably lucrative supplement to the theatre. Television was a long way down the scale of respectability but, as ever in that most precarious of professions, hunger concentrated the mind wonderfully. That traditional actors' problem, absence of work offers, meant that the chance to work, even in television, was too good to miss.

He was deeply aware of the way his early career differed from that his father had suffered, or enjoyed. 'Back in my father's day there was a normal progression for an actor's career. He could get his start on Broadway then a studio would take him over and mould his career. But when I went to New York in '68 there was no theatre. I did a little off-Broadway, then I made two or three pictures that didn't go. The studios don't put actors under contract any more so I figured the best way to move my career along was to get into a TV series.'

He developed a long-standing love affair with San Francisco and the city became an uncredited star of the series. Some of the breathtaking location shoots were very influential in bringing increased numbers of tourists to the city. Some of those locations also appeared twenty years later, albeit updated, in *Basic Instinct*.

The role as Steve Keller working alongside the craggy reliable brilliance of Karl Malden was an essential part of Michael's long-term education. A working rapport rapidly appeared and the pairing became one of the tightest, and most productive, on network television. The buddy show later became a cliché but the Douglas-Malden partnership still had something fresh and genuine to offer. It was also touching to see Michael Douglas acting with a man who was not only a contemporary but also a friend of his father. The links between Kirk and Karl Malden went back many years, back to their first steps in the business, for some of their earliest acting experiences were shared. Indeed it is thought that the name 'Kirk Douglas' was suggested by Karl Malden's wife during a period when she and her husband and the then Isadore Demsky were acting in a summer stock production together.

Michael Douglas was left with nothing but praise for the show. 'It was a great experience. We did fifty-two minutes of finished film in seven shooting days. Karl and I would finish a scene, grab the film cans and camera, hop into the truck and go off to another location. It taught me a very valuable lesson about film-making. If a show is going to work out everyone – cast and crew – has to work together.' This appreciation of teamwork is one of the many valuable things he would eventually take from the show. Many of his later comments on producing would come back to the importance of teamwork. *Streets* taught him that invaluable lesson.

Karl Malden was equally proud of the excellence of the show. 'The relationship of Steve and Mike – the old cop and the young one, the kidding around, the generation gap, which I think is one of the strengths of the show – is the way I am with Mike Douglas,' stated Karl Malden during the third season. 'If Mike Stone treats Steve with more respect now, because he's matured as a cop, I treat Mike Douglas with the same respect because he really has matured as an actor.'

The programme became a learning medium for Douglas who attracted great praise from Malden because of his willingness to learn. 'Karl taught you about listening. He taught you the strength of working with good people – there are actors who protect themselves by working with mediocrity so they can shine. I learned about structure and rhythm. I learned about producing. I directed a couple of episodes. I did 26 episodes a year with a guy who had a phenomenal ethic.'

The programme is recalled as a great success, but this didn't come immediately. Even though the series is fondly remembered and attracted legions of fans it wasn't a hit from the outset. The all-important Nielsen ratings were poor and for a time even the future of the show looked uncertain. It was one of those rare shows on American television which was allowed time to develop a style and a following. As Karl Malden admitted the show eventually became a hit because 'there are three stars of the series; Mike Douglas and me and San Francisco'.

It became extremely successful thanks to crisp scripts, imaginative use of outdoor shooting in San Francisco, and, most importantly, the interplay between Douglas and Malden. They developed a gentle mocking interplay which became a feature of the series and played heavily on the old stock theme of young stag versus old stag. It worked mainly because Karl Malden was sufficiently generous and creative to allow the young Michael Douglas the slack he needed.

'Even though I was comparatively new to the business Karl never gave me the feeling I was a beginner,' admitted Michael. 'Another star would perhaps have felt the threat of rivalry and tried to push me into the background. Perhaps it is because he knew my father from earlier days and played with him on the stage, but Karl is rather protective towards me, almost as if I were his son.'

Yet it took a polite objection from Douglas to the clearly subsidiary role with which he was initially saddled to make the part of Steve Keller a strong one alongside Mike Stone. 'In the end I told Quinn that I wanted out unless I had more to do. He was understanding and it has worked out so I have a show, Karl has a show, then we do one together. It's good for us, and good for the series.'

Quinn Martin was the major force overseeing the emergence of Michael Douglas as a star. 'Michael's got the potential to have a great future. When he's through with the series he'll be mature enough to get feature roles. He's been a great asset to us, and will be to anyone.'

His four years on *Streets of San Francisco* turned Michael Douglas into a star. He also received several Emmy nominations during the run of the show. His work brought him fame, and prosperity and recognition by his peers and, finally, acceptance from his father. It also brought Michael some satisfaction to become famous via television, one of the few areas not conquered by Kirk Douglas. The old competition between father and son wasn't ended by *Streets of San Francisco* but the success of the show marked the first tangible shift in the relationship between Michael and Kirk. For the first time Michael had a major success to set alongside those of his father, and even *Spartacus* had never been watched by thirty million people every week.

'The presence of a TV star in a movie can help the sale of a movie to television,' admitted Michael Douglas. 'When you're in a series that is watched by 30 million people once a week the impact is unbelievable. My father has been a movie star for years and when we'd go out together someplace he was amazed at the attention I'd get because of the series.'

The show made Michael a personality and a bankable face. As a television star in America any actor or actress becomes public property to an extent which exceeds the old glory days of Hollywood. A face can come to seem very personable and familiar when it hits your living room at the same time every week. This development came as a pleasant surprise to Michael but it was clearly a massive surprise to his father. Coming from an earlier generation of actors who had no real appreciation of the effects of television stardom Kirk was visibly unprepared for the totality of the stardom which had been visited upon his son. It was a pleasant awakening for Kirk, but it still caused a jolt. This shock was a kind of warning shot across the bows as Michael Douglas had other, more substantial shocks waiting in the near future for his father.

The work in San Francisco also brought Michael an unexpected bonus. On the programme they filmed 104 episodes at a rate of twelve pages of dialogue a day. The benefits were obvious to Douglas as he commented, 'They can throw anything at me after that and I've been there. I know everything, everything about production.'

Looking back on the years which covered *Streets of San Francisco* and later encompassed his first work as producer on films Douglas is clearly grateful for the experience. 'It took a couple of years to make the deal. By then I had had some production experience, having worked on *Streets* for four years. I only acted in the show but when you are an integral part of the making of a one-hour film every six days for four years, you can't help but notice how films are made. So that served me well.'

However, there was a downside and it came in his personal life. Brenda didn't like San Francisco. 'I'd die there. You've gotta climb hills, groceries have to be delivered,' she admitted candidly. 'I find it kind of provincial.'

Michael's enforced stays in San Francisco began to cause problems. The working and shooting schedule demanded a six-day working week which didn't leave a lot of free time. Brenda preferred living in Los Angeles in the large, comfortable house they shared in Benedict Canyon. She travelled sometimes to San Francisco. He returned more often to Los Angeles sometimes making the flight south down the Pacific coast in a rented plane. The flying lessons he had taken in the early seventies had brought him his pilot's licence and this added to his reputation as some kind of playboy adventurer. That reputation had been started by the commune period but was bolstered by the rumours of the exuberant way Douglas was enjoying his new fame and fortune in San Francisco. Those rumours obviously percolated through to Brenda back in Los Angeles and perhaps they caused the first slight cracks in their cosy relationship. Whatever the initial cause the pair had allowed themselves to begin to drift apart and their career concerns would exacerbate the situation. Brenda with her various television and film work; Michael with *Streets* and a new project which was taking up increasing amounts of his time.

4   A Cuckoo Out of the Nest

The next period of his life came to be dominated by Ken Kesey's political parable, *One Flew Over the Cuckoo's Nest*. This seminal book had long been associated with the Douglas family as Kirk had purchased the rights to the novel soon after its appearance in 1962.

Initially he planned on converting the book into a vehicle for himself to effect a Broadway triumph. He had become a major screen star with no appearances on the Great White Way since 1947, and there were many voices advising him to keep to the cinema. The lure of the book, and the central role of Randall P. McMurphy, was too strong and Douglas commissioned a stage adaptation by Dale Wasserman.

It went into New Haven for try-out before transferring to the Cort Theatre on Broadway. The reception in Connecticut had been enthusiastic and hopes were high for a long New York run and, ultimately, a film production. Kirk had always intended to develop the book into an important play and then film it, and those plans fermented over many years.

His eager expectations were never realized. The play enjoyed a satisfactory run but Kirk then encountered great difficulty in interesting any studio in the project. 'There was obviously a general conception of the book as a far-out, art-house piece' commented film critic Henry Rogers. 'Studios wouldn't risk capital behind a film about an asylum.'

Many years later the film would receive five Oscars and container-loads of accolades, and prove, yet again, the paucity of thinking in the hierarchies of studios.

Kirk spent so long fighting and arguing against the studio bosses, trying to persuade them that the film should be made, that he ended up tired and disillusioned from the effort. 'No studio would take a chance on doing it. Why I never knew,' he commented bitterly in a newspaper interview on tour with the play. 'I never thought of it as an arty film. It was a brilliant story, just on sheer dramatic value. After a while I got beaten down. You're fighting the system, but it's like the guy in *Lonely Are The Brave*. You keep on fighting the system and you're going to get destroyed.'

As a supreme, cruel irony he also grew too old to play the central role. The character of Randall P. McMurphy had to be fleshed out by a man who had not yet succumbed to the soft embellishments and quiet betrayals of middle age. There is an uncompromising savagery in McMurphy which quietly and imperceptibly slipped out of the grasp of Kirk Douglas as the years rolled by.

He grew uncharacteristically tight-lipped about the problems, but it became common knowledge around Hollywood that if the film ever got made it would not, could not, star Kirk Douglas.

'It broke the guy's heart,' admitted Charlie Fellows, a studio executive at the time. 'Here was Kirk Douglas, one of the biggest stars in Hollywood with the role of his life, and he couldn't get a studio to touch it!'

The opening of the play had provided an eerie echo of the problems of mixing Hollywood and drama. The play was staged at the Schubert Theatre in New Haven where, just across the street, the Sherman Cinema was advertising *20,000 Leagues Under The Sea* which also starred Kirk Douglas.

Eventually Kirk's business advisers convinced him that Kesey's play was a property which had to be sold. He let it be known in the movie community that $150,000 would secure the rights to the book.

There was no stampede to take the property off Kirk Douglas. In the end Michael persuaded his father that there was a chance of seeing the project through to fruition under his, Kirk's son's control. This was undoubtedly something of a gamble. Michael had no production experience and was still learning the business. No other greenhorn would have been entrusted with the power and responsibility of the production of a major Hollywood film. No other greenhorn without that vital family connection to the first owner of the rights, Kirk Douglas.

Had this been one of the black and white romantic comedies of the thirties, the type made immortal by Frank Capra, the plot for the next few months would have been fairly obvious. Michael would have quickly obtained backing and finance for the production, the film would have been made, and everyone would have lived happily every after.

But this was harsh commercial life, not celluloid fairy tales. Michael would get the film made, but it was a terribly hard, long road which would occupy five years of his life before the triumphant Oscar night.

He made several rueful, often bitter comments on the difficulties which were assailing the production. 'We were ready to go a year ago, but the rights were snarled in litigation,' he complained in 1972, referring to a suit launched by Dale Wasserman. 'We want to do the book, not the play. That's all cleared now.' Unfortunately this confidence was misplaced as it was more than two years after this comment before production started.

The incessant delays and problems which beset *Cuckoo's Nest* made Michael Douglas into a harder, more resourceful man. The first problem was, inevitably, money. Just as Kirk had discovered, no studio was interested in ploughing big money into a film about a lunatic asylum. Following his father's abrasive example Michael gave the establishment the finger and began to look elsewhere.

Having come up through the rock and roll generation he was aware of a world beyond the normal sources available to producers. He found success and financing riches by going outside the film industry and tapping into the new aristocracy of California. Rock music had thrown up a super-élite of performers and moguls who were mirroring the excesses of the Hollywood élite over the past half century. At one time it was the silent stars, Pickford, Chaplin, Fairbanks et al, who built fabulous homes on the west coast. Moguls like William Randolph Hearst then out-performed them by erecting edifices like San Simeon, but from the late fifties it was the brash newcomers in rock music who had the opportunity and the millions to display consummate lack of taste.

One of the new super-rich was Saul Zaentz who was the controller of Fantasy Records based in Berkeley. This college town north of San Francisco had become notorious as the site of college unrest during the mid-sixties. It also became an unofficial centre for the counter-culture or flower power movement, and much of that movement's power came from the music of the area.

Many of the top bands of the period had

emerged in San Francisco, mainly thanks to Bill Graham and his Fillmore Ballroom. Groups like the Grateful Dead, Big Brother and the Holding Company, and Santana developed local, then national followings and were quickly snapped up by major labels. More, smaller labels were also looking for talent and during the late sixties Fantasy had become one of the most successful of the smaller independent record labels. It was mainly thanks to John Fogerty and his band, Creedence Clearwarter Revival.

A string of multi-million selling singles like *Green River* and *Proud Mary*, plus a rack of gold and platinum albums, had brought vast wealth to Fogerty and to Fantasy Records. Saul Zaentz had also had his life greatly advanced by this prosperity and he eventually agreed to invest $2 million into the *Cuckoo's Nest* project. This was but the first step Zaentz would take into production. In later years his production company would be responsible for such important films as *Amadeus*.

It was also crucial to the progress of the project that Zaentz worked out of Berkeley, just across the bay from San Francisco. Berkeley had long been a student, radical haven and as such Kesey's book was one of the basic texts which became part of the sub-culture, along with such works as *Lord of the Rings* and the *I Ching*. As Michael Douglas was spending long days working in the city it was very convenient to cruise over the bridge at the end of a day's filming on *Streets* to meet up with Zaentz.

The first significant problem to be addressed by Douglas and Zaentz was the screenplay, and initially Kesey was favourite to produce his own adaptation of the book. Meetings were held and Kesey received the gratifying information that he would be on salary if he developed a screenplay, but would be eligible for a cut of the takings even if the screenplay was eventually produced by another writer.

Several meetings were held with the mercurial Kesey, and a distorted version of the screenplay was produced. It owed more to Roman Polanski and Sam Peckinpah than to mainstream cinema, but even a succession of rewrites failed to develop anything more marketable.

The Oscar-winning screenplay which appeared on film was eventually produced by Bo Goldman and Lawrence Hauben, but that was after several major writers had trailed in Kesey's wake. Such a lengthy process of rewrites wasn't unusual in Hollywood; eyebrows were raised at the fact that Ken Kesey wasn't able to produce an acceptable version of his own book.

Choice of director was surprisingly uncomplicated. By amazing chance both Kirk and Michael had unwittingly thought of the same man, Milos Forman.

Kirk had tried to interest Forman in the project years earlier but they hadn't managed to make contact. Kirk had sent a copy of the book to Forman in Czechoslovakia, received no reply, and assumed that the director was not interested. It was only years later that Kirk learned that Milos Forman had not in fact received the material. Michael chose Forman without discussing the script with his father and it was a major shock, and a sign of how closely their thought processes matched, that they independently decided that Forman was the man.

Douglas, Forman and Saul Zaentz made an unlikely but formidable trio. 'The signifying point of the three of us is we fought like hell. I remember many, many days we argued – and all of us remember it happily!' admitted Zaentz. This view is shared by Douglas who recalled that, 'We did everything wrong, yet everything right!'

The one missing element, the key to the film, was McMurphy. Once Kirk reluctantly abdicated his chance at the role his producer son had to consider an alternative. Names like Brando, Gene Hackman, and Burt Reynolds were suggested with varying degrees of conviction. James Cahn even turned down the part stating, 'I felt it was a wonderfully written thing but it wasn't visual. I didn't know Milos was going to do such a great job as he did!'

Fortunately for the finished film, producer Michael Douglas had an instinctive sense that Jack Nicholson was made for the role long before the script was ready. He watched a pre-release cut of *The Last Detail* with Saul Zaentz and Nicholson's bravura performance as Buddusky convinced both men that only Nicholson could play the part.

Nicholson had extensive commitments, notably to his work in *The Fortune* for Mike Nichols, but for once the interminable delays worked out to the advantage of *Cuckoo's Nest*. 'We'll finish our season on *Streets* about the time Nicholson finishes the new Mike Nichols film,' stated Michael Douglas. 'Some of this great crew of *Streets of San Francisco* will go to Oregon to work on the film.'

Salem is a small town south of Portland, the state capital of Oregon. It was there that location shooting had been arranged on *Cuckoo's Nest*, and the crew and most of the cast headed north from San Francisco into the wilds.

Nicholson arrived ahead of the rest of the cast and crew, putting into practice his legendary application and devotion to a role. He spent two weeks in the hospital immersing himself in the culture and the practices of the institution, and even managed to strike up friendships with some of the inmates. The research enabled him to get some understanding of the rigours of institution life and the deprivations felt by the unfortunates confined within those walls. It is perhaps difficult to believe in the wake of his Oscar-winning triumph, but he entertained serious doubts about his ability to manage the role.

Finally, fortunately, Nicholson was persuaded that he was able to infuse the role of McMurphy with that wild, magical energy which made the character so memorable. Ironically these were qualities which those fortunate to see Kirk's stage performance were able to recognize. 'Kirk was sensational in the role,' remembered Charles Fellows. 'Although one was a play and the other a film it would be hard to choose between Jack and Kirk as the definitive McMurphy.' Given such recollections it is particularly sad that Douglas was denied the chance of the film role.

Director Milos Forman was in an ideal position to recognize Nicholson's supreme talent. 'The moment he begins to work he becomes a servant: he knows the story, he knows the film, he arrives each day prepared to perfection, he is interested in an excellent ambience and he helps to create it.'

Forman was also particularly appreciative of one of the many surprise strengths of the film, Louise Fletcher as Nurse Ratched.

'Louise had the strength to do it subtle. She didn't go for cheap exaggeration. It was the most difficult part in the picture. I was afraid that, surrounded by all those spectacular performances, she would get lost.'

Louise Fletcher took the Oscar as Best Actress and few would dispute the choice given the withering power of her performance. Producer Michael Douglas was one of those deeply impressed by the intensity generated by Fletcher and he was among the first to leap to his feet in acclamation when she was named as Best Actress at the Oscar ceremony. Some, however, were less impressed.

Ellen Burstyn, winner of Best Actress in the previous year, went to the extraordinary lengths of appearing on television to ask academy members not to register a vote in the category of Best Actress. Her rationale was that all the actresses in that category had played supporting rather than feature roles, but there were many who saw Burstyn's move as a flash of vicious pique.

It was a triumph for Fletcher particularly as the role had been rejected by so many other actresses. Names like Anne Bancroft, Geraldine Page, Angela Lansbury and, not surprisingly, Ellen Burstyn were approached but turned down the part. 'Five actresses turned down the part of Nurse Ratched because she's an evil bitch,' stated Michael Douglas. 'In terms of being politically correct at that time, a woman couldn't play a villain. But for men it's always made their careers!'

This comment took on increased impact when seen against the events of 1987 when the 'nice' Mr Douglas suddenly appeared in *Fatal Attraction* and *Wall Street*. That was the point when he abandoned the nice guy, and often bland roles with which he had become associated. Playing a nasty changed everything for Douglas.

There was too much energy to be trapped purely on the *Cuckoo's Nest* film set. Many members of cast and crew were desperate to get away from the depressing surroundings of the institution and so Nicholson became pack leader, taking a troop of friends and associates and colleagues on boozy sybaritic jaunts into the towns around Salem after filming concluded each day.

A firm friendship was struck between Nicholson and Douglas, one which was to survive the filming and become enmeshed in legend as the pair took their libidos on a free-wheeling promotional tour for the film. Many of the more colourful details of certain of the incidents which littered that trip are still locked away in police reports. However, sufficient details escaped the tight, claustrophobic controls of the Public Relations machine to prove that both Douglas and Nicholson were healthy young men with a pronounced interest in the pleasures, and the sins, of the flesh.

One of the most endearing aspects of the younger public Michael Douglas was the way he invariably refused to hide behind the comfortable evasion or the vague platitudes which are the constituent elements of studio-speak. When asked about the promotional tour he was characteristically forthright. 'I went around the world promoting the picture and I enjoyed myself. I was single at the time, so I made every effort to savour the experience in the most decadent way. I think a few people were worried about what I was doing to myself. I got a little excessive.'

When the film was released it was an immediate, enormous hit. Of course it gained because it had a ready-made constituency. Millions had read Kesey's book since it was first published, and many readers were eager to see if the anarchic novel would translate accurately onto the screen.

Cuckoo's Nest became one of those rare, barnstorming films achieving massive commercial and critical popularity before dominating all the award ceremonies in its time.

Inevitably the Oscar ceremony in 1976 was dominated by *Cuckoo's Nest* with the film nominated for nine awards. The ceremony became a procession of people leaping onto the stage to accept awards for *Cuckoo's Nest*. It finally emerged with five of the film world's most prestigious accolades, and was the first film since *It Happened One Night* in 1934 to sweep away the five major Oscars. Since that time only *Silence of the Lambs* has matched that incredible level of success.

'I remember we were all sitting around after the Academy Awards – Milos Forman [director], Saul Zaentz [co-producer] and me – and I said, "Well, it's all downhill from here",' recalled Michael Douglas.

It didn't escape anybody's attention that Michael Douglas had got his hands on an Oscar before his legendary, acerbic father. Hopefully the $15 million reputedly earned by Kirk Douglas from *Cuckoo's Nest* helped to soften the blow. In his autobiography Kirk stated sadly, 'I made more money from that film than any I acted in, and I would gladly give back every cent if I could have played that role!'

'I will always be indebted to my father for *Cuckoo's Nest*,' admitted Michael Douglas, 'which happens to be the most important thing that happened in my career.'

The huge success of the film brought immediate fame and great riches to the younger Douglas. It also gave him the capacity to indulge in one of the Douglas family's favourite activities – revenge. 'Hollywood had long known that crossing Kirk Douglas meant that eventually he would try to get even,' recalled a columnist of the period. 'The first thing that *Cuckoo's Nest* showed was that Michael could enjoy dealing out retribution as thoroughly as his dad!'

All those companies and studios which had turned down Michael's approaches for finance were left to regret the fortunes they had thrown away. They also had plenty of time to contemplate the folly of upsetting a member of the Douglas dynasty. One of the rueful studio executives commented, 'Now suddenly there's two of the bastards to watch out for!'

Saul Zaentz didn't share this jaundiced view of Michael Douglas. 'There is a very considerate side to him – he went out of his way to do nice things without publicity. I always felt he had to prove it to his father.'

'What kept me going was the revenge factor,' gleefully admitted Douglas. 'That's a key part of producing. It's like "Someday, someday, I'm going to get that sonofabitch. I'm going to have a hit picture". I think revenge is a very good motivation if you can direct it. It's healthy. Very healthy. It's like, maybe you happen to be in a restaurant somewhere and see somebody, and you just stop and say hello, "Hi, I'm celebrating passing a hundred million dollars in grosses. Nice to see you again!" Revenge is great.'

The final words, even if humorously intended, have a chilling foretaste of Gordon Gekko's 'Greed is Good' speech, but that lay several years in the future.

And if the monumental success of *Cuckoo's Nest* signalled a major change in Michael's career it also marked a very significant change in his personal life. The long-standing romance with Brenda Vaccaro fizzled out. Not because of any disagreement, or any fresh relationship. The point which forced the split was simply that careers were moving in contrasting directions, and that they had become different people from the two comparative youngsters who had begun the relationship. Earlier problems about the amount of time he spent in San Francisco achieved greater significance and it became obvious that a separation was inevitable.

Brenda and Michael parted, without rancour, and went off to separate lives and diverging careers. Looking back it is clear that both of them in different ways were reluctant to commit themselves to any formal relationship. Brenda was usually reticent on the subject of her relationship with Michael but on occasion she did unburden herself.

Having marriage with bonds or anchors – the refridgerator, the station wagon – or having nothing are both extremes. I don't believe in either. I believe there's a middle. The middle is ecstasy. To reach it takes lots of time, because you can't do away with conditioning. It's the nature of the human being not to find the middle. So what I'm saying is that living with someone leads you to the same place. Freedom is only within yourself.

An unusually perceptive article in the *National Enquirer* in 1974 quoted Michael on the end of the affair. 'I was probably frightened about getting into something I just couldn't end by walking out the door.'

This apparent immaturity would slowly bleed out of him, and his future marriage to Diandra would benefit from the personal lessons he learned from his years with Brenda.

There was one poignant professional moment before they went their separate ways. Brenda worked on a film with Kirk Douglas and her work resulted in her receiving a nomination for an Academy Award. Yet again Kirk was overlooked as was the film, *Once is Not Enough*, and the snub hit hard. It must have been even more cruel when Kirk saw his son's live-in lover taking the accolades while his efforts were disregarded.

Such minor difficulties were soon forgotten once it became apparent that Brenda and Michael's relationship was finished. This sudden freedom left Michael free to pursue his bacchanalian instincts and he threw himself into his new life with unrestrained relish.

The ending of the relationship allowed him to immerse himself in a range of activities some of which had been on hold. A long-standing interest in politics resurfaced as part of the general fervour which arose after Watergate. Although Michael Douglas had resolutely refused to align himself formally with either of the main American parties he still displayed a sardonic distaste for some of the activities of the Republicans.

This was the time, post-Nixon, of heavy investigations, and general paranoia, and an era before it was credible that a mere actor could attain the highest office in the land.

Temperamentally Michael Douglas was a maverick and in the wake of Watergate there was no place for such animals in the Republican party. So it was in January 1977 that Douglas, accompanied by the ebullient Nicholson, travelled to the capital to attend the presidential inaugural ceremonies.

The celebrations revolved around the election of Jimmy Carter, the Democratic candidate, in November 1976, and Douglas and Nicholson were happy to welcome the arrival of a Democrat in the White House after the conspiratorial darkness of the Nixon years.

Both men went first to Kennedy Centre to attend a concert. This was followed by an exclusive white tie reception with the exultant Carter. Douglas and Nicholson were guests at the reception along with many other luminaries from the arts and entertainment worlds. One of the principal guests was Phil Walden, chief of Capricorn Records, who had been a firm and generous backer of Carter's campaign for the Presidency.

There was an uncanny parallel between the Carter-Walden relationship and that earlier one between Douglas and Saul Zaentz of Fantasy Records. In different ways both Carter and Douglas achieved something which many had thought impossible. They had made these breakthroughs at least partly by cleverly utilizing the financial bounty made available by local entrepreneurs grown rich from rock music.

The reception was the usual glitzy Washington affair populated entirely by the rich and the famous. Both Nicholson and Douglas were lionized by the mob but suddenly that didn't matter to Michael Douglas. In one of those blinding, unlikely moments of fate he fell hopelessly in love.

The girl's name was Diandra Luker. She was

nineteen years old, a resident of Washington D.C., and an embryonic member of the diplomatic service, studying at the School of Foreign Service at Georgetown University. She was also a member of a much more establishment family than the first-generation Michael Douglas. She inhabited a world of artists, and boarding schools, spending some of her early years on the island of Majorca where, much later, she and Michael would establish a holiday base. Exclusive people and the political intelligentsia were her circle. She had little contact with films or television, and unlike most people at the Washington reception she had no real idea who Michael Douglas was.

There was some slight justification. In the wake of his world promotional tour Douglas had grown a full black beard giving him a rakish, slightly piratical appearance. Even regular viewers of *Streets of San Francisco* would have been hard-pressed to recognize Steve Keller in the dark, almost threatening figure at the reception. Initially she presumed him to be an artist of some type, either painter or sculptor.

Douglas described his first sight of his future wife in delicate, touching terms. 'Across a crowded room I saw Diandra in a white dress looking like a Botticelli Madonna.'

Small talk began, slowly, nervously. He perceived her as an ethereal figure, but she saw him as altogether different. 'He had different perspectives about things . . . He was Sixties, rock and roll, and drugs. I had never heard of that. We were people from opposite worlds.' .

She had a date arranged for the following day. He eventually persuaded her to break it so that she could go out with him. Jimmy Webb, award-winning songwriter, is a long-time friend of Michael's and he has a wickedly cynical view of the hurried courtship of Diandra. 'Michael just stole her – typical!'

The flirtation passed rapidly into something more serious. Two weeks kept them totally together, and by then Michael was ready to ask Diandra to be his wife. It may have been a surprise that she accepted so readily but he was obviously besotted with the new woman in his life. There were suspicions at the time that, owing to the suddenness of the decision, that Michael was marrying on the rebound. After the comfortable domesticity with Brenda came a period of wild libertine bachelorhood. Now he was to revert completely in another direction and undertake marriage. To many people it just didn't make sense.

Jimmy Carter's inauguration was held in January 1977. Just two months later Michael Douglas married Diandra Luker. 'It sure surprised me, it was the last thing I'd thought of,' he admitted happily. 'I fell in love and I fell in love – for whatever reason – with a stranger. Diandra and I got married only six or seven weeks after we met.'

The wedding took place on 20 March 1977 at Kirk's house in Beverly Hills with guests like Nicholson, Warren Beatty, and Gregory Peck. Karl Malden, long-time friend of Kirk and early mentor of Michael, was also there but the ceremony was kept deliberately low-key. It wasn't a high-powered Hollywood wedding as the guest list was restricted to less than thirty. That didn't matter to the happy couple. It was obvious to all present that they were deeply in love and that they were planning a full life together.

They moved to Los Angeles where Michael planned to continue his developing career and Diandra joined the University of California. That new married lifestyle immersed her in a movie culture which was totally alien to her, and she, on discovering the complexities of his profession, was forced to state, 'I was shocked. But it was too late!'

Suddenly there were problems which hadn't previously been apparent. 'There was an experience gap,' admitted Douglas. 'We were both aware that if we didn't make changes, the relationship didn't have a chance.'

'She knew nobody,' he later stated. 'She felt she walked around in my shadow, while I buzzed around leading this wonderful, exciting life.'

It was a major change for both of them but Diandra clearly had to endure a greater degree of suffering. All her earlier experiences had been gathered in a quieter, less public arena than the one in which she suddenly found herself. Nothing could have prepared her for the new goldfish bowl lifestyle and it was obviously her feeling that Michael's sensitivity to her problems was less than it could have been.

Every new marriage encounters problems. The couple were faced with more than most mainly as a result of Michael's high profile and undoubted appeal for women.

They worked through the early difficulties to such effect that their first child, Cameron Morrell Douglas, was born just before Christmas 1978. This major change in their lives inspired them to make another move. Their period in Los Angeles ended and the family moved to Santa Barbara, back to the locale of Michael's commune period and to the location of one of Diandra's boarding schools.

However, business concerns led Michael to believe that he would be better in Los Angeles and the family quickly relocated to the city. Whilst there Michael immersed himself in a number of new ventures including the *Los Angeles Weekly* and the Committee of Concern. This was a quasi-educational body, sponsored primarily by those in the entertainment industry, which concentrated on developments in Central America. Diandra Douglas quickly found an interest in such activities and for a time she seemed content.

But this was illusory and her east coast antipathy for Los Angeles began to reappear. It was partly redeemed by a compromise settlement in Santa Barbara which enabled the couple to keep a base in California without having to be immersed in the claustrophobic confines of Los Angeles. The succession of moves between Los Angeles and Santa Barbara is proof of a certain restlessness and insecurity which would eventually be solved by taking a house in Santa Barbara and a separate domicile in New York. Before long the general distaste for California and all its wildness would lead the family back to New York. Prior to that Michael's acting, more than his producing, career received another very welcome boost.

Several years had passed since his early films and following the success as producer of *Cuckoo's Nest* there was a severe danger that Hollywood could forget that he was also an actor.

He played Dr Mark Bellows in the film *Coma* in 1978 with some success. Reviewers at the time praised his 'quiet authority' and his 'unstated sensitivity'. Sherry Lansing was obviously impressed by his work in the film. 'I remember seeing the dailies of *Coma* and thinking that combination of sexuality and vulnerability would make Michael a giant star!'

Other reviewers paid tribute to the fact that he had been prepared to play second lead in a major film to a woman, Genevieve Bujold. However, this apparently generous gesture was clearly influenced by the fact that he had little clout in the film world. Indeed at the time of *Coma* Michael Douglas was better known as a film producer than an actor, thanks to the runaway success of *Cuckoo's Nest*. He was remembered for his television work in *Streets* and for occasional plays but to the general public he meant nothing in films.

Coma was more successful as a book than a film. The screenplay curiously failed to capture the mood of quiet terror which permeates the novel. The performance delivered by Michael Douglas managed to keep his acting career in the state of ambivalence into which it had slumped. He got some good reviews but they were outnumbered by the bad ones or even the frankly apathetic ones. The film left his career neither going up nor down, just moribund, waiting for something to happen. The film was quietly forgotten and is only notable now for the fact that one of the bodies kept in suspended animation in the film was the soon-to-become Superman, Christopher Reeve. However, even the 'man of steel' was unable to shake off the atmosphere of torpor which spread across the film.

Director Michael Crichton, despite working on the screenplay and receiving assistance from author/doctor Robin Cook, was unable to realize the tension of the novel. It was hoped that *Coma* would exploit the increasingly important horror market, the territory which had produced a generation afraid to go swimming because of *Jaws*.

Sadly, the inherent weaknesses of the script, and some unresolved pieces of implausibility in the screenplay left the tension less intense than it should have been. The acting was generally competent but on the whole the film realized far less of its promise than it could have done. One of its few saving graces was the fact that it didn't slump into the obvious trap of concentrating on the gory aspects which the setting within a hospital offered.

The role of Mark Bellows offered Douglas the chance to become a simple jobbing actor once more. No concern for screenplay, or props, or any of the thousands of details which preoccupy a film producer. Robin Cook's novel was adapted for the screen by an ex-doctor turned writer and director, and Michael Crichton gave Douglas the chance to display a quiet earnestness and commitment. He was pleased with the project and commented, 'This is the first time I've been offered a project with a good story laid out well, a good cast, and a good director.'

If nothing else the film demonstrated his commitment to his work and this great attribute would become even more prominent in his next project.

5   The Career Grows

He then turned to *The China Syndrome*. This apocalyptic vision of the consequences of a nuclear accident appeared at a most propitious time. The green lobby was growing ever more critical of nuclear power, and the MUSE movement, Musicians United for Safety Energy, had started to grab major headlines and to seize the political initiative. Suddenly nuclear power and its attendant dangers were part of a much wider public consciousness. Then came Three Mile Island.

The infamous incident at the nuclear reactor in Harrisburg, Pennsylvania came in March 1978, just twelve days before the film was released.

Although nobody could have wished for such an accident its potential as a publicity exercise could not be doubted. The publicity men had been deliberating on the best way to exploit the message of the film. Prior to *The China Syndrome* few people were aware of the awesome potential for disaster concealed inside every reactor. People stumbling out of the theatres and cinemas after seeing the film were different. They had been educated in the harsh realities of the nuclear world, and for many the phrase, 'China syndrome', came to take on a new, sobering reality.

Publicity presented a problem. Massive budgets are allocated for publicity on major Hollywood films but, given the delicate nature of the subject matter, the tone of the projected campaign caused much heart-searching.

The studio decided to emphasize the ominous importance of the film. Their advertising announced, 'Only a handful of people know what *The China Syndrome* means. Soon you will know.'

The studio luminary in charge of advertising at that time was Jack Brodsky. Some years later he would abandon Columbia and join Michael Douglas' company, Bigstick Productions, as executive vice-president. When Three Mile Island became a national issue Brodsky decided that it would be a responsible move to keep the studio separate from the furore. 'We bent over backwards to disassociate ourselves from the situation. It was far too serious an issue to exploit.'

Unusually for the film industry the principal actors were ready to distance themselves from the publicity bandwagon, given the sensitivity of the subject matter in the wake of Three Mile Island. Jack Lemmon turned down an appearance on a CBS documentary special about the Three Mile Island crisis. Michael Douglas absented himself from a scheduled appearance on *The Tonight Show*. Jane Fonda, still carrying the torch for every radical cause, was less reticent. She held her own press conference to speak out about the nuclear issue but was sufficiently responsible to emphasize that the opinions expressed were her own, not those of the film.

Eyewitness to Power was intended to be the original title of the film. Mike Gray, because he had co-written the original script with Tom Cook, was initially scheduled to be director, with the full support of producer, Michael Douglas. There was one major problem with the appointment of Gray. His only previous film experience was in directing low budget documentaries, totally different from controlling a large budget film starring names like Fonda, Lemmon and Douglas. The only way to do such a film with Gray was to persuade the strong cast to take cuts in their normal fees. Everybody went for percentages but various members of the cast, particularly Fonda, were unhappy with Gray and eventually he was ousted.

Not surprisingly Gray was unhappy with the circumstances and especially the part played by Jane Fonda and her people. Gray didn't want it to be a Hollywood film. Because of the gravity of the subject matter he was concerned to adopt a darker, more documentary-style feel for the film. This didn't square with Fonda's view of a suitable vehicle for her talents. Faced with a choice between a major star and a largely unproven director there was only one route to follow. Gray was out, but the bitterness, particularly towards Jane Fonda, lingered. 'Although Jane Fonda is politically radical, professionally she is quite conservative,' snarled Gray.

The final director of *The China Syndrome* was James Bridges and his taut direction added greatly to the pace and power of the film. He was not a popular choice with Columbia Pictures and Michael Douglas had to battle with the studio to get Bridges.

This was a particularly noble gesture by Douglas as Jim Bridges had earlier turned Douglas down for a role in another film. Bridges had great regard for Douglas as an actor but, more importantly, as a man. 'Meticulous, dogged, totally creative . . . But most of all he's a lot of fun.'

Yet although Bridges was never hassled by Douglas the producer he was never left ignorant of the fact that Douglas was always wearing two hats. 'During one particular sequence Michael as producer kept nagging me, "Hurry up we're days behind. We've got to get out of here." I left, until the last shot, a close-up of him as star.'

The performances of the three principals were the hook on which the success of the film turned, but they were complemented by several consummate performances from a number of quality American character actors.

At one stage Jack Nicholson was considering an offer to play one of the two main roles but pressure of work compelled him to look elsewhere. The film gained because of the stature brought to it by Jack Lemmon's appearance as nuclear plant supervisor, Jack Godell. Yet it was anything but a conventional acting job for the peerless Lemmon. 'I stayed out of work a year to do this little mother,' he admitted. 'I'm proud as hell to be in the damn film.'

Michael Douglas was clearly proud of what *China Syndrome* was, and what it came to represent. 'I found this parallel with *Cuckoo's Nest*. Individuals caught in a corporate or social structure that forces them to make a moral decision at the sacrifice of losing their lives. It's an effort at what is basically Greek tragedy.'

He spent a lot of time telling anybody who would listen about his pride in *The China Syndrome*. 'I know this is a really good picture, but somehow I can't shake the feeling that if you tell someone upfront too many times how terrific something is they tend to have a let-down when they see it.'

He had much to be proud of in *The China Syndrome*, and much to bring him pleasure as both actor and producer. The film took $20 million at the American box office over its first weekend. That success, added to *Cuckoo's Nest*, kept him on a high in Hollywood and allowed the trades to hype the film even more.

It was the first time Douglas had worked with Jack Lemmon and he clearly enjoyed the experience, as he noted, 'Jack Lemmon is perfect in the film. He's a very unique guy. I kept thinking of him in *Save The Tiger*. When you keep him straight and simple he gives some wonderful performances.'

For his own part Lemmon was deeply impressed by Michael Douglas. 'What I love about Michael is he finally got *Cuckoo* off the ground and made one of the great, great films. He's bright, he's talented, but mainly he cares. That son of a bitch came up to my house and he was passionate. That was the film he wanted to do.'

Lemmon's usual immaculate performance drew plaudits from everyone. Even the acerbic John Simon commented, 'And the plant supervisor in *The China Syndrome* in his agonizing dilemma very nearly becomes a genuine tragic hero. Jack Lemmon trenchantly portrays this unspectacular man's rise to great moral heights as well as his ultimate collapse: no one can convey specious cheerfulness better than Lemmon or make you feel more clammily sweaty under the collar.'

Jane Fonda wasn't even scheduled to be in the original film for her part was originally written to be played by a man. Richard Dreyfuss was lined up for the part but personal problems, not unrelated to expensive white powders, led to his turning down the part. The role was then rewritten for a female lead and Jane Fonda was engaged to play newswoman Kimberley Wells. That basic rewriting allowed the film to address another important issue, the trivialization of news and the absence of women in important roles in television.

In the early part of the film Kimberley Wells is restricted to handling soft, entertainment-based items like animals' tea parties. Thanks to the happy coincidence of her being present at the plant when the first 'accident' occurs she becomes involved in the story and finally is the pivot on which the true story of what happened at the plant turns.

The film was an emotional experience for Fonda. She had become involved in the furore about the nuclear issue long before the project was even suggested to her. She had also tried to buy the rights to the tragic story of Karen Silkwood. That film eventually appeared with Meryl Streep in the lead role.

Fonda lost out in that battle but of the two films dealing with the nuclear issue it is *China Syndrome* which remains most starkly in people's memories.

Jane Fonda also suffered a good deal of abuse from workers at the facility used for filming the scenes inside the nuclear station. The film company had delicately misled the utility company about the purposes of filming. There was a perceived fear that the film would emerge as some biased anti-nuclear treatise but the film company calmed those worries and reassured the facility that no bad publicity for the nuclear industry would follow from the film.

Naturally this was a careful lie and all would have been well until a mischievous reporter leaked a copy of the shooting script to the workers at the plant. Inevitably all hell was let loose, and most venom was directed at Jane Fonda. At that period she was at the height of her powers as Red Jane, the so-called Communist sympathizer and anti-American harridan. Once the plant workers learned what the film was meant to do they turned against the film and the crew, and most virulently against Jane Fonda.

'The last few days filming were pretty hairy,' recalls one of the crew members. 'Jane came in for some bad treatment.'

The reaction from the plant workers came mostly in the form of verbal abuse. Fortunately the threats of physical violence were not realized but there were many expressions of muffled satisfaction when, during location filming, Jane Fonda slipped down a gully and fractured an ankle.

One important element absent from the film was a romantic involvement. Given the structure of the film and the relationships involved the obvious pairing for a romantic liaison was Douglas and Fonda. It didn't happen but Douglas wasn't at all surprised. 'Well, given where Jane Fonda was then and where I was as an actor it was not in the pecking order for me to have an affair with her.'

Michael Douglas was billed below Fonda and Lemmon but his urgent playing of cameraman Richard Adams pushed the film forward. It was this role which crystallized his public image as a good guy acting against massive, often inhuman forces, and it also showed the sardonic, self-mocking personality which became a major part of his appeal.

This persona would re-emerge in later films like *Romancing the Stone*, and enable Douglas to achieve a level of popularity which would attract women without alienating men. A few actors have achieved this feat and Michael Douglas can stand comparison with the likes of Harrison Ford and Sean Connery.

That developing personality was reinforced by the next film to appear, *Running*. Given the peculiar workings of the film industry it is perhaps no surprise that *Running* was finished almost a year before *The China Syndrome* but was actually released later.

The film didn't attract the same success or fame as *The China Syndrome* and in truth it didn't deserve to. *Running* was poorly scripted, emotional bilge, notable for a contrived ending *à la Rocky*. Given how poor the finished film was it is disturbing and a little astonishing to learn that

Douglas thought the original script was wonderful. 'I cried when I read it. I must have read hundreds of screenplays looking for something like this. The problem was to find a screenplay that really touched me in some way – dramatically, comically. I did *Coma* because it scared me; *Running* moved me!'

However moving Douglas thought the screenplay was the film failed to realize the potential he saw in it. It was voted one of the worst movies of the year in 1979 and several critics thought it was lucky to even make the list.

Running had just one saving grace – its credible and authentic athletic scenes which were helped in no small part by Michael's fanatical devotion to getting physically fit for the part. He trained rigorously for the role, lost over a stone in weight and undoubtedly looked good in his runninig scenes. 'I had to get in shape for it and it wasn't easy,' admitted Douglas. 'I haven't been in such good shape since school.' As Michael Andropolis the marathon runner he was very convincing but sadly the script didn't provide enough meat to enable him to flesh out Andropolis as a man.

The rest of the film failed to live up to the promise of the action scenes. Its general lack of purpose and conviction were clear to most reviewers and the film failed to advance the career of the younger Douglas.

The film's promoters were hoping that *Running* would gain at the box office from association with the increasingly popular jogging craze. It was also expected that the film would benefit from connections with the forthcoming Olympics. Sadly for the publicity machine the next Olympics was the ill-fated Moscow Games which were boycotted by the United States and others because of the Soviet invasion of Afghanistan. Lots of careers suffered because of the boycott; great athletes who had spent years training for one peak moment, one chance at the gold prize. In that context the problems suffered by one slight film seem trivial indeed.

The next venture undertaken by Douglas, *It's My Turn*, didn't improve matters. Cast as a baseball player forced to retire at a young age by injury Douglas brought a faint sense of brooding anger and resentment to the role but the film was not a commercial success. His main involvement in the film was to feature in a cold, bleak relationship with his new stepsister who was played by Jill Clayburgh.

The film was a weak, poorly resolved piece of work in which most of the principals seemed quite disinterested in what was happening. For his part Douglas stumbled through the role with little conviction and scant passion. It was not a piece of work in which he could take any real pride; it was more a case of acting-by-numbers, and it showed.

In his defence it must be said that there were more glaring holes in the film. On the surface it promised to be an intelligent analysis of relationships but, once again, Michael Douglas suffered because the screenplay failed to meet the challenges of the subject matter.

He suffered even more because of a dispute which arose after the film. Called upon to provide interviews as part of the promotional exercise for the film he declined. One of the gossip columnists of the period reported that Douglas despised the film and had refused to have anything to do with it. 'I never said that,' complained Douglas bitterly. 'What I said was that I couldn't shoot my wad like I did with *The China Syndrome*. I am overexposed. I told them I was willing to do some interviews, but not to count on me for all the talk shows. I am an actor, and I cannot go out like that after every film. That's what I said.'

He has always been one of the most accessible Hollywood stars in terms of the promotional needs of his films, and it was particularly cruel that the misunderstanding over *It's My Turn* led to some people in the industry calling him a prima donna. Douglas never has acted in such a selfish manner but the incident hurt him, both professionally and personally, and he did not deserve the reputation as an egotist that the débâcle of *It's My Turn* brought to him. It would be several years before that reputation would vanish.

It would seem that Michael Douglas gained only as a person from the film. It was directed by

Claudia Weill, and this fresh experience of being directed by a female caused Douglas to reconsider some of his more chauvinist views. Not that there was any vast explosion of pre-feminist feelings; Michael was still too much his father's son for that, but the undoubted influence of Claudia Weill certainly induced changes, beneficial changes, in Michael Douglas. In later years he would enthusiastically advance the cause of female directors but prior to his work with Claudia Weill he was not one of the most fervent advocates of women in the industry.

'I just loved having the director come up to me, put her arm around my shoulders and ask if I'm okay,' commented Douglas. 'She made me feel confident.'

Many years later he would confirm his belief in the power of women to affect the film industry and to effect beneficial changes. 'I look to women and blacks as our directing salvation – Penny Marshall and Martha Coolidge and any number of other wonderful women directors getting a chance.'

The draining experience of *It's My Turn*, added to his earlier endeavours on *Running* and *The China Syndrome*, caused Douglas to take the first of his intermittent extended breaks from acting. Tiredness was certainly an element but there were others. The immediate distraction of his young son, Cameron, was an obvious example of things which kept Michael from the camera. The presence of a new son was a massive inducement to stay home, and in a touching way the presence of Cameron brought Michael and Kirk even closer together. Being able to spend time with his grandson clearly delighted Kirk, but that time also became surrogate time for the years he hadn't spent with Michael or the other children.

And the chance to hold, to take some quality time with his own offspring caused Michael to reconsider some of his more inflammatory statements about his father. Cameron became the instrument which brought Kirk and Michael closer together, and since the birth of the child the bond between Kirk and Michael has grown ever tighter.

Another factor keeping Michael Douglas off-screen was the unmistakable fact that he was not exactly in demand as an actor. Scripts were offered, but in no great profusion, and he had to reconcile himself to the fact that little was happening in his career. 'I was just putting along as an actor. I didn't have any great parts. I was a little angry about it.'

His career has followed a roller-coaster course since the start but this period definitely represented one of the low points.

One useful result of the sabbatical was an increase in his power as a producer. It didn't escape the shrewd Michael Douglas that at that stage studios were far more interested in his prowess as a producer than as an actor. Columbia

Pictures agreed a three-year deal under which they would finance Michael's semi-independent production company, Bigstick. The deal covered all salaries and normal overheads and provided a satisfactory rate of return for Douglas for any films made during the period of the deal. It was at this point that Douglas engaged the services of Jack Brodsky, and thereby ruffled a few more feathers.

Brodsky had worked for Columbia for several years and there were a number of quiet accusations of poaching made against Bigstick and Michael Douglas. However, given the massive success and incredible revenues coming in the wake of *Cuckoo's Nest*, Douglas the producer was clearly seen as a major investment for Columbia. And in the world of big investment, matters like loyalty are of small consideration. The chief of Columbia Pictures, Leo Jaffe, commented that under the deal both Columbia and Bigstick were 'looking for pictures we can mutually agree upon'. There was no firm commitment to a schedule of filming but Douglas was heard to speculate that he was looking to develop a film a year. No specific projects were mentioned which was not a surprise.

During the four years following the signing of the deal not one film was completed, or even started, by Bigstick.

And yet this was not a fallow or idle period for the company. In the film world projects can be in development for many years before filming commences. Frank Price, then chief of Columbia Pictures commented, 'We had *Tootsie* in development for four years. If you're trying to make exceptional pictures (which is what Michael, all of us, are trying to do), it takes time.'

Bigstick had several projects under consideration including the purchase of a novel entitled *Virgin Kisses* written by Gloria Nagy. There was something in this story of a Beverly Hills dentist's passionate obsession which appealed to Michael Douglas, leading him to option the rights for Bigstick. Yet it would be almost eight years, and some three million words in rewrites, before the book would transmute sensationally into the film, *Fatal Attraction*, which would finally establish Michael Douglas as a major sex symbol and box office star of the eighties.

The first Bigstick production to result in a completed film was a Jeff Bridges vehicle, *Starman*. The release in 1984 provided the world with an engaging, thought-provoking film based on an inter-planetary visit to earth. The film featured an alien stranded on earth trying to make contact with his friends and effect a return home. Before that return can be effected the visitor has to evade the clutches of the harsh, unfeeling authority figures on earth, and in this he is aided by a lone earth character.

Unfortunately this well-constructed tale offers too many parallels to Steven Spielberg's *ET* and suffered calamitously because of the comparisons inevitably made by critics and the audience. In that respect *Starman* was most unfortunate. All concerned at Bigstick and Columbia regarded *Starman* as a love story which happened to have a science-fiction background. Comparisons with *ET* were played down, and the Bigstick/Columbia alliance were content to rely on the perceived strengths of their film. Unfortunately the delays on *Starman* meant that Spielberg was able to release his film first, and *Starman* was all but forgotten in the understandable rush to praise *ET*.

ET was a cultural phenomenon and nothing comparable could have flourished within its shadow. It is a matter of regret to all concerned that *Starman* as a project was under way long before *ET* was conceived, but *Starman* is now remembered as a pale imitation of the much more successful *ET*. In the list of top-grossing films of all time *ET* is proudly in the top group; *Starman* would be struggling to make the top one hundred, and yet there is much to admire in the John Carpenter film.

So much that for a time Douglas was seriously considering taking the main role himself. Politics dictated otherwise but it was a fascinating prospect.

Douglas, in his role as chief of Bigstick, was intrigued by the basic premise of the film. 'The wonderful idea of this woman showing the alien the absurdities of our planet and not meaning to do so. Everything in the world made sense except human behaviour. I liked the concept.'

Starman was generally received well by the critics but it didn't strike a chord with the public. Its respectable showing was a disappointment to the studio and to Bigstick Productions, particularly after the struggles to bring the film to completion. Difficulties with screenwriter and director meant that the schedule stretched almost into infinity.

Filming was scheduled to begin in October 1982 under the direction of John Badham but he changed his mind and abandoned the project. The initial script by Bruce Evans and Raynold Gideon was then pushed into a second draft and the project entered into a long series of rewrites.

Hollywood professional Dean Reisner came in as writer, unaware that he would spend over two years struggling with the incessant demand for rewrites. The industry buzz about *ET* left Reisner with an almost impossible task, made even worse by pressure from Columbia to deliver the product.

At the same time the list of directors offered and rejecting the project grew to farcical lengths. Michael Mann, then Tony Scott, then Adrian Lyne refused the job. Finally John Carpenter, fresh from such gentle, lyrical pieces as *The Thing*, *The Fog* and *Halloween* came in as director.

He then became embroiled in a major conflict about the film when he listed Dean Reisner as co-screenwriter. The dispute went to arbitration at the American Writers' Guild but the finding came down in favour of the original writers, Gideon and Evans. When Carpenter deliberately included a dedication to Reisner in the film credits the Writers' Guild took the move as a deliberately provocative violation of their ruling. For a short time the Guild were threatening to force Columbia to destroy all copies of the film containing Carpenter's offending dedication to Reisner.

Such unpleasantness would not have mattered had the film proved a massive success but it didn't. In many circles *Starman* became famous solely as the film which Columbia made instead of *ET*. Universal took *ET* and Columbia hung on to *Starman*. *ET* took hundreds of millions of dollars at the box-office: *Starman* made less than a tenth of the revenue of its more illustrious cousin, and the mud stuck with everyone involved including Bigstick.

It didn't seriously damage Michael's reputation as a major producer but suddenly the lustre created by *Cuckoo's Nest* was dimmed. It didn't help that his acting career was less than glowing at that period.

A severe skiing accident then led to a serious virus condition affecting his blood. This situation dragged on for several months and led to a prolonged absence from acting. In the end three years were to pass between *It's My Turn* and his role as an idealistic judge in *The Star Chamber*. This mature analysis of the perversities of the judicial system was co-written by Roderick Taylor and Peter Hyams. It showed Douglas as a young judge who finds himself growing disillusioned by the failures of the legal system. He grows appalled and frustrated by his obligation to free murderers, on technicalities, when he is convinced of their guilt.

Other judges on the circuit recognize his fury and invite him to join and then initiate him into a secret society known as The Group. This clandestine assembly then act outside the law to inflict vigilante-style justice on wrongdoers. This is a theme which has appeared, in a more substantial fashion, in a number of films, most notably the Clint Eastwood epic *Dirty Harry*.

The film also seemed to suffer because of its marketing stance. The time of its release was firmly in the period when the teenage audience took over the cinemas demanding an undiluted diet of escapist entertainment. *Star Chamber* was perhaps the wrong film at the wrong time. In an attempt to salvage some commercial return the company ran a series of expensive television commercials promoting the film. Quite misleadingly the commercials concentrated on, and indeed exaggerated, the vigilante violence of the film. It was perhaps justice that the film failed, but whatever the mistakes of the merchandising people the failure of the film put another blight on the acting career of Michael Douglas.

Under a growing cloud he turned his attention to the third production being prepared by Bigstick. This was a project involving a script Douglas had purchased in 1979 from a waitress named Diana Renee Thomas. The script had been prepared in the limited spare time she could take from her restaurant job. She then submitted the screenplay to the usual weary round of readers and agents. It was her immense good fortune that Jack Brodsky came across the first draft, saw something in it, and passed it on to Michael Douglas. Within a week Douglas paid $250,000 for the script which would eventually become *Romancing the Stone*.

6 Romancing

'*Romancing* took a long time because people would not understand that you could juggle adventure, comedy and romance,' admitted Douglas in frustration. 'People kept saying "What is it?" I'd say, "Well it's an action adventure picture, it's a comedy, it's a romance." They'd say, "You can't do that. What's the concept?" And so I lost a lot of time.'

This was an old-fashioned romantic adventure, in which the hero and heroine brave a number of hair-raising exploits before escaping to a new life together. As such it came out of a rich tradition of swashbuckling films featuring such legendary characters as Errol Flynn and Stewart Granger.

One of the principal differences between *Romancing the Stone* and earlier films was that it featured the heroine so prominently and sympathetically. For obvious reasons that reflected both the dispositions of its original writer and the mood of the time. Diana Thomas was far from being a strident feminist but she did produce a lively, witty script which featured a real woman in an active lead role, and this was far from normal in Hollywood.

When he reflected on *Romancing* Michael Douglas had firm views on the strengths of the film. 'Do I think, in hindsight, that I should have protected or developed my part more for *Romancing the Stone?* It made Kathleen's career. She became a big star after it, but the picture was about her character. *Romancing* was about the growth of a woman, a young woman going from this to that, meeting this guy, and the adventure she had. It was her story!' admitted Douglas. 'If we had screwed around with that I wouldn't have made myself a star because the picture would have been a turkey. And stars are made out of pictures that are successful.'

It is a matter of record that several actors turned down the role of Jack Colton because of the prominence given to the female lead. Robert Redford and Harrison Ford were considered; Sylvester Stallone was offered the role before rejecting it, and it was only as something of an afterthought that Douglas agreed to both produce and star in the film.

His casting for female lead and second male lead appear in retrospect to be inspired. To play the part of Ralph, the diminutive quasi-gangster who follows hero and heroine across Columbia, Douglas turned to an old friend from his early days in New York. Danny De Vito had come through the American Academy of Dramatic Arts before scuffling around New York in the search for work. His friendship with Michael Douglas was established in those impoverished days. When Douglas saw him in an off-Broadway performance of *Cuckoo's Nest* the memory brought Douglas to offer him the same role in the film.

The ensemble playing in *Cuckoo's Nest* was one of the film's strengths. The inmates in the institution who are provoked and galvanized by Nicholson feature some of the cream of American character actors, but two future stars were concealed on the ward. Christopher Lloyd, later to become a huge hit in *Back to the Future* was there as was the diminutive Danny De Vito.

The offer of the role of Ralph to De Vito in *Romancing the Stone* was not motivated by kindness or friendship. De Vito's sly, maniacal energy was perfect for Ralph and his performance greatly added to the overall attraction of the film. There was an innate charm in the side-by-side playing of the dumpy De Vito and the handsome Douglas, and it is possible that the germ of the idea which eventually became *Twins* came from *Romancing*.

The choice of female lead proved more difficult. Once again entreaties were made to a number of leading actresses without success. Eventually the name of Kathleen Turner was suggested to Michael by Joe Wixan, the production president at 20th Century Fox. She had just come off a spectacular hit as the sultry *femme fatale* opposite William Hurt in *Body Heat*. Her smouldering performance caused Douglas to doubt whether she could bring sufficient wide-eyed innocence to the role of Joan Wilder. A meeting in Burbank, followed by a deeply impressive screen test, convinced Douglas that his doubts were ill-founded and Kathleen Turner got the part.

A couple of personal points may have helped her selection. Like Diandra, Michael's wife, Kathleen Turner came from a family in the diplomatic service, and she had spent long periods in South America, the chosen location for *Romancing*.

'She knocked him sideways, no doubt about it!' remembered Sally Grunwald. 'Douglas really didn't think she was right for the role, thought she was too obviously sexy, but the screen test persuaded him that he was wrong, and Kathleen became Joan Wilder.'

Another key element was the choice of director. For that pivotal post Michael Douglas went for a young film graduate of the University of South California named Robert Zemeckis. This was his first major directing commission at the age of thirty-two but it would lead to many others, particularly the record-breaking *Back to the Future* trilogy.

Zemeckis was just one of the future stars of the film world who received an important assist from Michael Douglas. He could have picked a more comfortable setting for his first location job. However, it was one of those situations where so much happened that all those involved, particularly producer and director, learned immense amounts. It proved a gruelling but invaluable learning experience.

In a revealing television piece Douglas described his ideal director, and thereby explained why Zemeckis got the job. 'I've liked to work with directors who are hungry, who want opinions, just so I would have a voice. I didn't feel comfortable working with big-time directors. I'm just not happy with that style – the shouters, the hollerers, the tyrants.'

Zemeckis had already made impressive waves in the film world. His first film, *Used Cars*, was a spectacularly tasteless black comedy involving the antics of car dealers anxious to sell their products. Although not a great commercial success the film attracted interest and plaudits for Zemeckis. His reputation was also helped by an involvement with industry whizz-kid Steven Spielberg who, impressed by an early demo from Zemeckis, had commissioned Zemeckis and his co-writer Robert Gale to produce a screenplay for his film *1941*.

Zemeckis had little work offered to him following *Used Cars* and so he wasn't in a position to refuse the approach from Michael Douglas. Within a week producer and director were in Mexico investigating locations for the film.

Location shooting was scheduled by Douglas to

begin during the summer of 1983. He had finally settled on Mexico rather than Columbia for financial and logistic reasons. Costs were lower in Mexico, it was considerably closer to California and the weather was expected to be less inclement. Also Douglas had to choose a location which would provide the terrain described in the screenplay without causing major financial problems.

Unfortunately the locals had misinformed Douglas and the crew about the problems that the weather could cause. The film crew were promised sunshine with just a slight chance of rain. General assurances about a probable rainfall of half an hour a day proved hopelessly optimistic. In fact the *Romancing the Stone* production ran into a greater level of rainfall than at any time in the previous forty years.

It became an exercise in damage retrieval for Michael Douglas, and the admiration of his cast and crew for his calm competence is unchallenged. 'Michael seemed to be on top of every situation,' recalled Kathleen Turner. 'If a road washed out and we couldn't get to our location, the next morning there were thirty dump trucks full of gravel waiting to lay in that road. We were building Douglasland all over Mexico.'

The prospect of Michael and Kirk emulating Walt Disney and constructing their own memorial is appealing, if a little terrifying. Fortunately it didn't come to that.

The crew worked frantically to complete work on the film and the level of co-operation between them and their producer was obvious to all. One crew member has vivid memories of Douglas at work.

He's tough but he makes decisions and he knows exactly what he wants. If you have a problem you go to him – he knows what you're talking about, and he'll give you a decision. A lot of them in this business are tough and totally useless. A lot of them I can't find for a week. Michael wasn't always Mr Nice Guy – but he was always there. He called me a son of a bitch – I called him a son of a bitch, but as a producer he's as good as any. He's got all the things you can love and hate in a person!

Kathleen Turner remains convinced that Douglas the producer succeeded at the expense of the actor. 'I'm not sure he ever gave himself the indulgence he should have as an actor.'

Michael Douglas had to concentrate all his energies on the supreme challenge of chiselling a major motion picture out of a jungle. The problems which dogged the shooting of *Romancing the Stone* were incredible. An alligator severed one of the hands of its trainer. Pre-determined locations would have vanished by the time the crews arrived, carried off in landslides or washed away in torrential floods. There was even one memorable occasion when the second unit crew arrived to set up shooting only to discover that the beautiful scenery in the remote valley had disappeared beneath the waters of a newly-formed lake.

The non-stop rain even presented Robert Zemeckis with an unusual and amusing problem. Much of the film included scenes set in rainfall and storms but he realized to his horror that real rain doesn't register like ordinary rain to the film cameras. The units were left in the miserable position of having to wait around in the constant downpours for the rain to stop so that the crew could bring in some fake rain. Interviewed for CBS television Zemeckis wryly observed, 'We ended up having to make all our own rain for the scenes. We'd get all wet and miserable waiting for the real rain to stop so we could start our phoney rain.'

It is a matter of human experience that people who have endured a gruelling or painful experience can, eventually, laugh about it. Time heals, or so runs the old saw. In that respect it is curious that virtually all those who suffered through the location shooting for *Romancing the Stone* cannot speak well of the experience. The pain, the misery, the sheer discomfort is still too vivid for laughter, even after several years have passed.

Possibly the epitome of the saturated madness was the climatic image of the film, the wonderful mudslide scene. The clip in the film is a mini-masterpiece of timing, thrills and fun with Turner and then Douglas cascading down the dissolving mountainside. It ends with Turner spreadeagled in a fetid pool of water only to find Douglas flying in to land face-down between her legs.

It was a wonderful piece of cinema and its potential for promotion was quickly recognized by Douglas the producer. That single clip appeared constantly on television and cinema screens to alert audiences to the exciting possibilities of the film. *Variety* reckoned that more people saw that single clip than had seen the top ten grossing films of all time!

And yet those huge audiences could never realize what great turmoil was involved in filming those few seconds of action. Naturally the stars, particularly Turner, were too valuable to risk and so hard-working stunt doubles were brought in for the filming. Jeannie Epper was Turner's double, her latest job in a long line of doubling for such stars as Linda Evans, Shirley MacLaine and Angie Dickinson.

Her work on *Romancing the Stone* was far more arduous than anything she had previously undertaken. Although handsomely paid, and the recipient of the 1984 Most Spectacular Stunt Award, she was brutally explicit about what the scene cost her in bruises and damaged pride. 'It was awful. Hundreds of gallons of water knocking us over, down through this sea of freezing mud into a dirty pool. The glamour of filming!'

The other members of the cast and crew also suffered. Even Zemeckis lost more than twenty pounds in the course of the production whilst Douglas, borne down by the twin pressures of acting and producing, lost weight and gained an unhealthy grey pallor.

The impact of shooting a marathon in a jungle had long-term effects on Zemeckis, and for years afterwards he would speak ruefully of the experience. 'It was hard on your mind, your clothes, your spirit and your body. But I survived!'

With all the problems, all the monumental difficulties, it wouldn't be surprising if everybody involved with the film rushed to disassociate themselves once filming was concluded. In fact there was a common perception that a first-class piece of work had been produced, and consequently few of the principals were surprised when the film turned out to be a hit. It was a surprise hit which also delighted the accountants. Douglas and Zemeckis managed, despite all the obstacles, to bring the film in below $10 million and it would eventually gross over $100 million in cinema takings alone.

As a supreme irony that windfall did not go to the coffers of Columbia Pictures. The three-year deal between Columbia and Bigstick ended and, despite overtures, Michael decided not to renew it. *Romancing* had proved to be one of the stumbling blocks; the long delays in development, following similar problems with *Starman*, made Columbia question their involvement with Bigstick. That hesitation persuaded Michael Douglas to end the connection.

'The Columbia deal was not a good business deal. I discovered I work best in a funky little office with just a reader and a secretary,' admitted Douglas.

When *Romancing* finally reached the cinemas the logo seen as part of the opening credits was that of 20th Century Fox, and that company gained greatly from Columbia's loss.

The film gained from the earlier success of *Raiders of the Lost Ark* – indeed Zemeckis is on record as stating that *Stone* would not have been made if *Raiders* had not already appeared. Yet the differences between the two films are sufficiently pronounced to make each stand alone as a viable piece of work. Similarities indeed, but the differences are far more pronounced and numerous.

Douglas became a one-man promotional bandwagon for the film and he dragged the mudslide clip to every notable chat show and interview programme he could find. He even appeared as guest host on *Saturday Night Live*, the infamous American television comedy programme and managed to insert three plugs for the film within an hour.

Douglas received a number of offers to exploit the merchandising possibilities raised by the film's success. The prospect of Jack Colton action dolls or Joan Wilder lunchboxes may be beguiling but, patently amused, Douglas spurned all the approaches.

With such a commercial blockbuster there was inevitably pressure for a follow-up. And there was also the undeniable fact that the public clearly liked Jack Colton and Joan Wilder. Market research indicated that there was a demonstrable interest in what had happened to them after they had sailed away down 5th Avenue to begin their round-the-world cruise.

20th Century Fox began to make noises about a sequel within weeks of the release of *Romancing* but no commitment was made until the figures appeared on the balance sheet. Those figures were so glowing through the late summer of 1984 the decision was taken to go for a sequel, and in September Michael Douglas was asked by Fox to produce a second film by Christmas of the following year. This was, in fact, a frightening request. It would have been a demanding schedule even if the production wheels were turning but at that stage there was nothing, not even a script or story outline, in place. Douglas was being asked to launch a major production and bring it through to final print stage within a mere fifteen months. For any film this was an intense workload, but for an action film like *Jewel* requiring a great deal of location shooting it was an insane schedule.

The other principals in *Romancing* had moved on to other projects and growing success. Kathleen Turner's reputation had been made by her work in *Romancing the Stone* and she began to consolidate a career which would exalt her in Hollywood. Zemeckis gained a little weight, and took up writing again with long-time partner Robert Gale and their new collaboration produced one of the biggest ever Hollywood hits, *Back to the Future*.

For Douglas the plaudits for *Romancing* weren't as numerous or as prominent. The role of producer/actor is thankless and the poignancy of the sitution was brought absurdly home in the wake of the success of *Romancing*.

In the interim period between *Romancing* and *Jewel* he took another simple acting job, but used the period to set up the production on *Jewel*.

That next job took him well away from the production duties which had drained him so severely during the filming in Mexico. He accepted the role of Zack, the choreography director, in *A Chorus Line*. The original musical had become the longest-running show in Broadway's history with a clutch of touring companies also taking it out across the country.

The universal appeal of the work was obvious. *Chorus Line* was an icon of the American musical theatre gathering a Pulitzer Prize plus a clutch of Tony awards for the original cast.

Michael Douglas responded to the challenge of appearing in a piece which was already well established without suffering the artistic rigours of having to create something fresh. It was also important that all the filming was to take place in New York which meant that he didn't need to leave home to complete his work in the film. Perhaps that unusual degree of creature comfort compromised his efforts for his performance seemed curiously lack-lustre, especially compared to the energetic power he generated as the buccaneering Jack Colton.

Part of the problem was possibly distraction. During the filming of *A Chorus Line* he began to work seriously and even frantically on the myriad preparations for the sequel to *Romancing* which would be *Jewel of the Nile*.

He took office space in the Mark Hellinger Theatre where *Chorus Line* was being filmed and worked on conversions to the working script for *Jewel*. The first draft had been prepared by Mark Rosenthal and Lawrence Konner to a brief suggested by Douglas. He then worked on rewrites during the long periods when he was not required for filming at the Hellinger Theatre. It was situations like this which foisted an unfortunate reputation on Douglas. An impression was created and widely spread throughout the industry that Michael Douglas was a man who always wore more than one hat.

By any standards that was unfair. Most film

actors and actresses complete their scenes and then disappear rapidly to the privacy of the luxury trailer. Once hidden in such a cloistered environment such stars are free to pursue any number of interests or perversions.

Michael Douglas chose not to do that. While he was on call in the Hellinger Theatre but not actually required for filming he chose to work. That worried Hollywood, and his reputation suffered accordingly. That false impression still dogs him and has caused great embarrassment and irritation. It came to a head on the set of *Wall Street* and was only resolved by a deeply searching conversation between Douglas and Oliver North.

'People think of Michael as doing a piece of acting while he's got a phone in one hand fixing up some production deal,' laughed a crew member. 'It's not that bad, but the truth isn't so different!'

The final day's shooting on *Chorus Line* overran dramatically and the crew, and Douglas, worked through the night. Rather than join in any celebration party or prolonged festivities Michael Douglas took a cab to J.F.K. Airport to catch on early morning flight to Morocco.

After such an epic journey, especially following directly on from an all-night shoot, he could have reasonably expected a peaceful and troublefree time in Morocco. Unfortunately the plane deposited him in the middle of the biggest production mess of his career. In a delicately appropriate phrase Michael described himself as being 'in deep shit' and events proved that he wasn't exaggerating.

Morocco had been chosen over a number of alternatives, but Mexico had not even been considered. Memories of the floods and the jungles and the rainfall were still too strong, and there was a discernible yearning for a location shoot somewhere warm and dry. Morocco relieved of the blistering heat of the summer seemed an ideal setting, and Michael, the producer, had made his usual advance preparations.

'Lewis Teague had been set as director because Bob Zemeckis, the director of *Romancing*, wasn't available. We all met in England to decide where we were going to film. It appeared that Egypt was sort of dicey and spread out, and they didn't have everything. Israel didn't have everything. We could shoot part of it in Morocco and part of it in Israel. I was a little nervous about that. I didn't foresee getting many long-distance telephone calls through to Morocco from Tel Aviv because of the whole Arab-Jewish situation. So we decided on Morocco.'

When Douglas finally flew into Morocco he came expecting to find an infrastructure in place which would enable him to impose the logistic support for a major motion picture. Instead he found chaos. Location sites hadn't been organized, equipment hadn't been hired, and the crew awaiting his arrival comprised just two locals.

When he, not unreasonably, asked where the rest of the crew could be found he was told that they were in Nice. The production assistant advised Douglas that Nice was a good stopping-off point, and couldn't understand the look of disbelief which crossed the producer's face.

There were major decisions to be taken but first he deliberated on whether 20th Century Fox should be informed about the débâcle which had greeted him in Morocco. There was even a serious debate about whether the whole project should be abandoned. The studio was banking on the completed film being available for the Christmas 1985 season. Such a tight schedule left Douglas with little spare time and any delay in filming would prove disastrous.

His feelings at that moment were grimly expressed in a telling quote. 'I heard this screaming voice inside me shout, "Here you go. Life's been real good. You've been waiting for someone to do something really bad to you and this is it"!'

In panic, fear and desperation Michael turned to those he could trust, and he immediately phoned his brother Joel virtually commanding him to get on the next plane to Morocco. As Joel had acted as co-producer on several Michael Douglas productions there was a level of trust between the pair which transcended the family

119

bond. Joel's calm reliability and implacability were to prove invaluable in the frenetic madness of Morocco.

Acting in concert the two brothers began to inspect and organize all location details, and Joel put into operation the frantic process of importing all the necessary equipment and hardware for filming. Michael flew back to California to put some more work in on the script and to complete the crucial job of casting. Because of the chaos which greeted him in Morocco he had been forced to put aside all thoughts of casting. Lewis Teague was consulted, briefly, but the first occasion on which Michael Douglas could spare the time to look at the options for casting was on the jet taking him back over the Atlantic.

At that stage it was intended, naturally, that the film would be built on the established personalities and characters from *Romancing*, and so it was a bombshell when it was revealed that Kathleen Turner was refusing to do the film. The problem was not money nor the role she was being asked to play; Turner had taken exception to elements within the script which, in her judgement, rendered the first draft of less impressive standard than *Romancing*.

'It wasn't that I ever intended not doing the sequel,' she later stated. 'I just wanted *Jewel* to have the same quality as the original, and I felt that what I had been given was written in the wrong spirit. Women writers are different than

120

An early action shot of a youthful Michael Douglas in *Hail Hero!* (1969)

The aggressive young actor in *Coma* (1978)

The old hand and the newcomer, Karl Malden and Michael Douglas on the *Streets of San Francisco* (1972)

Michael Douglas with Jack Lemmon and Jane Fonda in *The China Syndrome* (1979)

Michael Douglas and Kathleen Turner become acquainted in *Romancing the Stone* (1984)

Troubles beset Michael Douglas as Jack Colton in *The Jewel of the Nile* (1985)

Michael Douglas as New York attorney, Dan Gallagher, finds his weekend fling turning into a horrendous nightmare in *Fatal Attraction* (1987)

Glenn Close meets Michael Douglas and wife, Anne Archer, in *Fatal Attraction* (1987)

Michael Douglas and Charlie Sheen live dangerously in *Wall Street*
(1987)

Michael Douglas as the ruthless
Gordon Gekko in *Wall Street*
(1987)

Kathleen Turner, Danny De Vito and Michael Douglas in *The War of the Roses* (1989)

Michael Douglas and Melanie Griffith as lovers in Nazi Germany in *Shining Through* (1991)

Sharon Stone and Michael Douglas share an intimate moment in *Basic Instinct*

men. They were writing jokes I didn't find funny, like having the Africans drag Joan off into a hut.'

Quite understandably Kathleen Turner was using some of her new-found industry muscle to carve things to her liking. The first film, *Romancing*, had made her a huge star; by wanting her for the sequel 20th Century chiefs were forced to concede a much higher fee, plus points, and were compelled to listen to her demands.

She had also expressed an interest in appearing in *The Money Pit*, a new Steven Spielberg production which would overlap with *Jewel of the Nile*. Perhaps she would have done it; perhaps she wouldn't. Conceivably it was just a bargaining ploy, a lever to use against 20th Century Fox to demonstrate to them that she suddenly had clout in the industry.

The 20th Century Fox luminaries weren't impressed by Turner's stand and in response they handed her a $25 million lawsuit. Eventually, with a laudable amount of co-operation, the script problems were settled and Turner rejoined the team. Douglas worked on in Los Angeles, ploughing on through the minutiae of pre-production work only to be bitterly halted by a real tragedy out in Morocco.

The production designer, loction manager and their pilot disappeared while out scouting locations for the second unit filming. Their plane was missing for four days before it and the bodies were found. Douglas was still in California having delegated duties in Morocco to the invaluable Joel but he was clearly torn between the need to stay in California and complete pre-production work and the entirely understandable desire to fly to the site of the tragedy.

His personal dilemma was exacerbated by the fact that the 1985 Academy Awards ceremony was imminent. He had to attend the ceremony for business reasons but it was hard to press the flesh and smile when his project so many thousands of miles away seemed dogged by problems and tragedies.

We were set to start shooting in April. I went back to California to work on the script, to do casting. I would do the Academy Awards and then leave the next day to go back to Morocco. And when I got back there was the whole thing with Kathleen. About a week before the awards I get word that we'd lost our production designer, location manager and pilot in a crash. That was a very, very sad time because they were missing for four days. It was hard for everybody.

I didn't know whether to go over there. My brother was telling me, 'We're doing everything we can, you've got to keep going ahead with the script. There's nothing you can do here!' he continued. But it was a very, very uncomfortable and sad time, trying to continue with the picture, having meetings, and you kind of drift off for a while and look out a window, and out there somewhere they're still missing.

Some of the crew toiling away in Morocco

began to feel that the film was cursed or fated, and several men actually left the site for that reason. After the tragedy we lost a couple of people who just wanted to leave the picture because they felt it was doomed.

Michael and Joel were too committed, too close to the project to indulge such fears. Instead they ground doggedly on with their respective tasks although they were still 7000 miles apart. It became a massive consolation to Michael Douglas that the man holding the reins in Morocco was not an employee or a hired hand but his brother.

Things improved temporarily in April when Michael returned to Morocco. At that traumatic point he discovered that he had walked into another hornets' nest. Like so many other factors the accommodation arranged for location shooting had proved insufficient for the numbers in the crew. In desperation Michael Douglas requested that people should double-up temporarily. Some people, often unfairly described as the English contingent, refused and the result was a massive row which ended with a number of people, including the production manager, being sacked. The expression used by Michael Douglas for what happened is brief and highly charged. 'I cleaned house!' and witnesses liken it to the turmoil when Christ threw the money-lenders out of the temple. 'Michael's rage was amazing, and a bit frightening' remembered one observer.

Not for the first time the steel at the core of Michael's practised geniality was exposed. There were those who thought of him as a soft touch, a rich playboy. Such doubters who characterized him in such a disparaging manner were disavowed quickly and painfully of that impression.

Shooting became a nightmare sufficient to make the veterans of the earlier film think back nostalgically to Mexico. There was a multitude of problems with the weather, but even more difficulties caused by the graft and corruption which provided the foundation for the bureaucracy through which any film set has to work.

The need to bring in huge amounts of fake weaponry for the film caused immense complications. Bribery opened some doors but quite frequently it was necessary for Michael to display some of the famous Douglas truculence to get results.

Some things were beyond his power to control. Thousands of posters had to be destroyed and rewritten hours before being used. Inadvertently the original had been written containing a spectacular Arabic profanity.

Production designer Terry Smith erected an ambitious set in the desert. The chosen area had suffered a calamitous drought for over six years. Shortly after building work had finished on the castle, the centrepiece of the site, the rainfall started. It poured non-stop for more than a week, and that was simply unprecedented in that region.

'If it had happened two thousand years ago,' moaned Smith, 'it would have made the Bible. Something in the Atlas Mountains gave way and a wall of water eight feet high swept down through the dry river bed. In fifteen seconds everything we hd struggled to build was washed away!'

Filming in Morocco was not a happy process. Problems with the script, difficulties with the various locations, misery and illness among cast and crew – all contibuted to the general malaise.

If there was relief among the crew at the ending of filming for *Romancing* in Mexico there was near-ecstasy at being able to get out of Morocco. By that time illness and disease were rife among the cast. Hepatitis, dysentery, sunstroke, cholera and a mild form of malaria hit almost everybody and nobody was reluctant to be heading for France.

Michael Douglas has never been an overtly emotional man, at least in public. He has always tended to keep his deeper emotions buried rather than make violent demonstrations of feeling. For that reason the tribute he paid to those working on the film was all the more heartfelt.

The whole movie was like a battle. It was a war, but in the end, we were intact. Every day it was attack, attack, attack. But we started getting a pride going, and everybody was helping one another out. They were reaching out more than you normally would, even when you're tired or sick. And that's what you hope for. That's the magic or chemistry that as a producer you hope for. Because then you've got something that nobody can take away from you. You've got family, you've got stories, you've got memories. It makes me doubly glad the picture worked out. This is one where they can wear their T-shirts proudly!

There were equally abiding memories of Douglas left in some of his colleagues. 'He's full of charm and humour, but don't ever cross him! He's a very strong man – with the accent on strong – and had to claw his way out from under his father's giant shadow,' commented Kathleen Turner. 'I was glad that he didn't direct at the same time . . . As it was, I really had his attention when we were in the mud together.'

The problems on the shoot grew ever more intractable and a weariness settled on cast and crew with the temperatures consistently up beyond 100 degrees and the range of afflictions hitting the film-makers.

Departure from Morocco came with a bang, in the organized ebullient style for which Douglas the producer had become famous. He brought in two planes, a Boeing 737 for the cast and crew and a C-136 transport plane, loaded all the equipment and personnel on the planes and headed north. 'That was one of the nicest moments, knowing we were headed for France,' he later admitted.

As the cast and crew dissolved back into their own lives the Douglas brothers headed for London to commence editing the film and work on the soundtrack. Final edit was scheduled just five weeks ahead which meant that Douglas had to work intensely to complete the oral side of the project.

Facilities at Battery Studios were far more comprehensive than in Morocco and working conditions were infinitely better. The choice of sound and music was his alone, and the sessions produced yet another nugget as a promotional tool.

Nobody can now recall how or when the idea to use Billy Ocean's 'When The Going Gets Tough, The Tough Get Going' in the film. It was a masterstroke, as was the video later filmed by Douglas, Turner and De Vito in which they lovingly resurrected the old Temptations style of Tamla performance.

The Billy Ocean record prospered on the back of the film, and the hugely popular video, and became a hit all over the world with sales eventually reaching five million.

After all the difficulties during the long process of filming and editing there were more than a few Fox executives surprised to find Douglas able to deliver the film on deadline. It was released in early December 1985 but failed to raise the same excitement as the first Colton-Wilder adventure. Critics were less than complimentary, and box office returns also indicated less enthusiasm for the sequel.

This time the film was projected as a vehicle for Jack Colton far more than Joan Wilder. The various performances received fulsome praise but the film was generally lambasted as little more than a special effects and stunts vehicle. And the continuing adventures of Jack Colton failed to ignite or excite the population. As a result this directed more attention on to Douglas. 'It's about the growing up of Jack Colton . . . of the two as a couple,' admitted Douglas. 'Colton is a guy who's always on the move. When the going gets rough he's always ready to take off. He has to recognize just how much he loves this woman and what sacrifices he'd be willing to make.'

Michael Douglas was made to suffer more than most because he was forced to endure two critical maulings simultaneously. Richard Attenborough's film version of *A Chorus Line* was released just a few days later than *Jewel* and Michael's prominence in both films brought him more readily to the critics' attention than perhaps he deserved. As the focal point of *Jewel* and a key player in *Chorus Line* he was too prominent to be ignored by the hungry critics.

The glowing reviews he received for his work on *Romancing* were not repeated. The reviews for his performance in *Chorus Line* were even less pleasing. It was a bleak period in his career, and his professional disquiet was mirrored in one of the periods of estrangement from Diandra.

The draining effect of his work on *Jewel of the Nile* added to the reaction to that film and *Chorus Line* led to another apparent withdrawal from active involvement in the business. He pulled back, concentrating on the backstage activities of the producer where projects are in development over long periods of time. There was also a necessary period of rebirth with his family. Cameron was growing fast and the frequent rumours of strains in the marriage between Michael and Diandra could only be quelled by spending quality and extensive time together. The separation after the release of *Jewel* was painful and both Diandra and Michael agreed to work towards rescuing and renovating their marriage.

Life has an ironic way of imitating art, and vice-versa. The tribulations which were afflicting the marriage between Michael and Diandra had been around for some time. Her trips to Mexico with Cameron to visit the set of *Romancing the Stone* were not just for the scenery!

The period after the release of *Jewel of the Nile* and *A Chorus Line* saw Michael Douglas in rehabilitation with his family. There was no denying his devotion to his son, nor his love for Diandra but it seemed at times as though he wanted, needed more. Even his flourishing business empire seemed insufficient to satisfy the strange hunger inside him.

His disaffection was made worse by the lack-lustre reception for both of his recent films and the suspicion that he was in danger of over-exposure. For both reasons he felt it politic to withdraw for a while from his normally high profile life, and this was just the precursor to his later policy of taking a year or two off after a back-to-back project.

He made his intentions plain. 'I dream of being here in New York in January and being in my bathrobe for about four days. I do that. I just go pre-natal, and I get up early and I see my kid, and I have breakfast with him, and I look out the window a lot.'

This conventional, even boring, lifestyle clearly means a lot to him particularly as it provides a complete alternative to the high-pressure world of Hollywood films. But this time, while he was lounging around New York, he received the green light for the project which would change his status in the industry irrevocably.

7 *A Famous Attraction*

Almost two years were to pass before the release of his next film and the *angst* afflicting his personal life clearly spilled over into the film. It was to become the film which finally established Michael Douglas as a star to rank with his father, and become one of those rare films which capture and indeed mould the mood of an age. It was *Fatal Attraction* and after that film the casual fling by a married man would, could never be the same again.

The ideas which became *Fatal Attraction* had been in Michael Douglas' mind for several years. Having read Gloria Nagy's book, *Virgin Kisses*, he took it as a property for Bigstick and it was under consideration as a potential film project during the early eighties.

I found a book I liked. It's really a great book called *Virgin Kisses*. It's about a bored Beverly Hills psychiatrist who's seen everything. He cheated his way through medical school, got the right wife, a good practice. And a woman comes into his office. A pleasant-looking woman, but not your Beverly Hills normal-type thing. And there's something about her that drives this man crazy. It's about lust. It's about how a man destroys all his ethical practices and codes and starts hypnotizing, and his practice falls apart, and he's just gone. Everything's gone. Anyway, it's a book I tried many years ago to develop, but I couldn't get anybody interested. They'd look at me like I was crazy!

The interview which produced these telling admissions came in late 1985, two full years before the film appeared. It demonstrates just how long some properties can be in development before making it to the screen. Several of Michael's greatest successes have been years in preparation, and the relative lack of success of rushed projects like *Jewel of the Nile* argue that a lengthy development process can be genuinely helpful.

The words expressed by Michael Douglas also significantly indicate that the original impetus of the book/film was a study of male obsession. Somewhere in the constant rewrites the gender changed so that the woman became the protagonist.

The catalyst which moved *Virgin Kisses* from an interesting book to a viable film project was a chance conversation between Douglas and Stanley R. Jaffe on a plane trip between New York and the West Coast. Inevitably such a conversation between two people in the same business revolved around mutual interests and industry gossip. Likely projects came into the discussion and the *Virgin Kisses/Fatal Attraction* property was certainly in that category. Michael Douglas would have had no reluctance to speak about a potential project with Stanley Jaffe for the man had worked for many years as a co-producer with Sherry Lansing, one of Michael's most loyal friends. During the filming of *Fatal Attraction* Sherry Lansing spoke of him in one of the promotional interviews. 'I consider Michael a dear friend but most of my relationship with him is work-orientated.'

The Lansing-Jaffe partnership had achieved a position of strength and influence in the business, and both had spent their lives in the film industry. Stanley Jaffe's father, Leo, had worked in the business, most notably with Columbia, for almost fifty years. Stanley had moved into the film industry with such success that at the young age of twenty-nine he was running Paramount. For her part Sherry Lansing was the first female head of a major film studio, 20th Century Fox. She achieved even greater success after leaving 20th Century and moving into independent production. Her achievements included *Fatal Attraction* and *The Accused* among many others.

And there was little reluctance to depart the corporate life and end her three years with 20th

Century. 'It's a job that you can never really win at. The best thing you can hope for is a draw. You're only as good as your last film.'

The initial chat between Michael Douglas and Jaffe then developed into a more formal discussion at a meeting which also included Sherry Lansing once the pair had been confirmed as producers of the film. There was one significant problem confronting the producers and Douglas. It was inescapable fact that the original book portrayed the male lead, Dan Gallagher, in a distinctly unpleasant light. This was understandable given that the book was written by a woman, but that feminist slant cuased distinct problems.

For a major motion picture it was essential that that perception were softened. This modern morality tale would have victims and attackers, winners and losers but it couldn't be a simple black and white story. If Dan Gallagher were to be the naïve victim of the story he had to have a human edge to allow the cinema audience the chance to empathize and identify with his dilemma.

The machinations around the script began to assume almost mythical importance with the need to project the three lead characters as vital, credible people locked in a memorable struggle for ultimate survival.

In an effort to meet every commercial requirement the final version of James Dearden's screenplay was changed to include an alternative ending. Both were filmed, and both endings have since been seen by substantial numbers of people. Britain was initially offered a different conclusion to that in America and Japan but all areas saw the Glenn Close character die. The sheer power of the film's closing scenes was reinforced by the death of the deranged Alex, but even that element came to be a massive talking point. Arguments raged about Alex and Dan and their affair, particularly about the way the situation was resolved in the film.

Fatal Attraction became, quite simply, a phenomenon; a cinematic event which spawned discussion and debate, and even a profound examination of lifestyles. Producer Stanley Jaffe commented, 'We didn't set out to make a heavy message picture, but *Fatal Attraction* has certainly touched a chord.'

Douglas himself was staggered by the reaction to the film. 'I've never before been involved in a picture that emotionally hits people like this,' he admitted. 'Women are dragging their boyfriends or husbands to see it. It's sort of unrelenting.'

Director Adrian Lyne was equally bemused by the impact of *Fatal Attraction* on the public. 'I wasn't prepared for how much of an audience-participation movie it was going to be.' After the film had been on release for a few weeks Michael Douglas enthusiastically noted, 'They're going nuts in the theatres. People scream, they get hysterical. This is what making movies is all about.'

In a world suddenly conscious of Aids the consequences of a casual night's dalliance by Dan Gallagher took on a massive importance. Women and men across the world were thrown into angry confrontation about the roles of the two sexes as portrayed in the film. Attitudes were examined, and sides taken, and few people who saw the film could remain ambivalent about the various characters and their actions. The torrent of publicity created by the film was a dream for a publicist, and it must have been particularly satisfying to see the interest aroused by a mere film.

The torrid sexuality of *Fatal Attraction* came as a surprise, particularly in the new light it cast on Michael Douglas and Glenn Close. Previously both of them had been respected within the industry, but *Fatal Attraction* suddenly, and perhaps unexpectedly, made both of them into stars. The success of *Romancing the Stone* made Michael Douglas into a bankable property but, perhaps amazingly, *Fatal Attraction* turned Douglas and Close into sex symbols.

Douglas himself was surprised by this unlikely development, and yet he could see the stark similarity between himself and Dan Gallagher. This became such a potent force behind the success of the film, for the script carefully depicted Dan Gallagher as Everyman. 'I think

Fatal Attraction was the closest to who I am. I remember first looking at the script and saying, "Wait a minute, I could have been him!" I had to strip away at myself for that!'

After a series of bland or relatively simple films it was an interesting career move for him to move into something with a harder edge. Perhaps *Fatal Attraction* gave him his first opportunity to explore the darker side of human nature, a topic which continues to fascinate him. 'I'm interested in people who are flawed. They've all got a dark or degrading truth or edge to them,' commented Douglas. 'That's the reason I like to do them. I'm attracted to things that are real.'

The role of Dan Gallagher brought something out in him as an actor which hadn't been manifest on the cinema screen previously, at least to most people. Perhaps it was the weakness of the various screenplays with which he had been associated; perhaps it was due to his lack of development as an actor. *Fatal Attraction* found him making a breakthrough.

Sherry Lansing saw something else in Douglas which was a significant element in the success of the film. Against all expectations he managed to make adulterer Dan Gallagher a sympathetic character. Lansing first realized this, and the importance of it at a test screening long before the film was released. 'This man has an affair, and he comes back after the weekend and messes up the bed, so that his wife will think he slept in it. Well, the audience laughed – and I turned to Stanley and said, "They'll forgive him anything!" '

Douglas touched a nerve in many of those who saw the film by creating a sense of powerful, wounded vulnerability about Dan Gallagher. Despite the violence and the terror permeating the film it is difficult not to have some feelings for Gallagher. The man is a louse, but Douglas manages to make him a sympathetic character. Where Kirk and Michael share the same facial appearance with its undeniable cruelty Michael's is always tempered by sensitivity. This is a man capable of inflicting pain but this is also a man who has suffered.

Critics agree that it was Adrian Lyne as director who was able to draw elements from Douglas which few people had previously suspected. 'I always wondered why I never saw on film what I saw for real,' commented Lyne. 'He's a vulnerabale man, but he always played macho. In this he plays a loser and it was a real conflict for him to reveal that vulnerability. He kept saying – "Lemme do something!" '

Lyne was also deeply impressed by the depth of emotion presented by Glenn Close. 'When she and Michael tested, an extraordinary erotic transformation took place. She was this tragic bewildering mix of sexuality and rage – I watched Alex come to life.'

The sexual content of the film was sometimes graphic, occasionally shocking, but it was integral to the story and its central theme of obsession and compulsion. There is something squalid and disturbing in what Douglas and Close do to each other, for this isn't love, nor even passion. It is gratification without thought for responsibilities or consequences. In a world where an epidemic of biblical proportions was brewing, often as a direct result of the kind of unsafe sex portrayed in the film, the liaison between Douglas and Close had chilling overtones.

Adrian Lyne kept a frantic tempo building particularly in the scenes involving intimate contact between Close and Douglas. Initially she is the only character driven by wildness but then Douglas and eventually his screen wife, played by Anne Archer, are caught up in the madness, and it becomes a flame which consumes them all.

It was a realistic madness which was but one of the reasons why the public identified so closely with the predicaments faced by the characters. The intensity of the emotion was relieved at key points by wholly credible lighter moments such as the sight of Michael Douglas staggering round Glenn Close's kitchen with his trousers round his ankles. This seemingly was a character point introduced by Douglas himself and it is such moments which make Dan Gallagher a tragic but totally believable character. Adrian Lyne was impressed by the lightness and certainty of touch Douglas brought to the film. 'He doesn't have a sense of his own dignity, which is terrific!'

The film races on towards its inevitable conclusion. At one time some eight different endings were under consideration, and one of the prevailing strengths of Lyne's film was the way it caused people to argue about alternative endings. In fact in response to the downbeat feeling about the original ending expressed at the previews Jaffe and Lansing insisted on an alternative ending being shot, and cast and crew were brought back to complete the work.

Dawn Steele was president of production at Paramount when the studio first learned that the sample audience had reacted badly to the final scene in the original version of the film. 'You heard the whispering. You heard the letting out of air, almost like they had been holding their breath for two hours and then the end was disappointing for them.'

The initial ending emulated *Romeo and Juliet* with the star-crossed lover ending her life when she couldn't have her love. Bringing the story completely into the eighties the film had Alex commit suicide but leave sufficient clues to implicate Dan Gallagher in her death. The alternative, more commonly seen ending, has Alex seeking to wreak revenge on Dan and his family leading to a gory, but more pleasing, conclusion.

Paramount met all expenses for the reshooting and were delighted with the results. The film became the third-highest grossing film of 1987.

On virtually every level *Fatal Attraction* was a triumph. It brought back the culture of intelligence, thought-provoking adult films as an antidote to the diet of mindless teenage pap which seemed to be what the film industry believed the audience wanted. It also re-established the film culture which allowed serious film-makers to work on entertaining but mature pieces featuring adult characters in tense situations.

The publicity bandwagon surrounding the film was given greater impetus with a real-life incident which eerily mirrored the storyline of the film. Carolyn Warmus went on trial for the murder of Betty Jean Solomon, her former lover's wife, and those events brought *Fatal Attraction* into even greater focus.

The film presented the public with three powerful, credible characters who could find fervent and often fanatical supporters among the audience. Members of the American Academy were equally impressed with the impact of *Fatal Attraction*. Glenn Close was nominated for an Oscar as Best Actress and Anne Archer also received a nomination as Best Supporting Actress. Many people were surprised that Michael Douglas wasn't also nominated.

Perhaps the most crucial aspect of *Fatal Attraction* was that it was the first important film to appear after the dread of Aids had been presented to the world. As such it had an impact and an influence far beyond that of a mere film.

It was difficult to believe that Michael Douglas had been fortunate enough to be involved in two major films, *China Syndrome* and *Fatal Attraction*, which so perfectly captured the mood of the time. It defied belief that he could be so lucky again.

And yet *Wall Street* managed that amazing feat. It was a film which managed to capture and encapsulate the sense of materialistic greed become fashionable which so dominated the eighties. When the grasping, insensitive eighties are remembered it will be *Wall Street* which, for most people, summons up most distinct images of what the decade came to represent.

China Syndrome came out within two weeks of the disaster at Three Mile Island. *Fatal Attraction* opened at the time of deepest gloom about the spread of Aids in the heterosexual community. *Wall Street* appeared within weeks of Black Monday on the real Wall Street, when thousands of investors were ruined by the vicissitudes of the stock market and the actions of the financial wheeler-dealers.

The eighties was primarily the decade when greed became acceptable, when the traditional versions of the Ten Commandments and the seven deadly sins were resculpted by men in designer suits. In that climate the creation of the odious character, Gordon Gekko, was ideally suited to its time. The dictionary defines a gecko as a lizard which preys on small animals and never blinks its eyes. It is also able to achieve the unlikely feat of being able to scuttle up vertical surfaces.

Michael Douglas played Gekko with a cold selfishness which justified the dictionary definition and allowed the character to display and even epitomize the ruthlessness which had become grimly fashionable during the decade. He defined his reasons for wanting to play Gekko, the character who had suffered 'an ethical bypass at birth', in a TV interview.

'It's boring to play good guys. It really is. You look at most stars that made it. That one part where they play a bastard. People find it very attractive – women are attracted to someone who's bad. It's a very interesting thing; they like a little nastiness.'

Gekko was bad; rich and powerful and totally amoral. As such he was a compelling and unforgettable creation.

Douglas proved correct in his assessment of the relative values of nice parts and nasty parts for an actor, and he had a convenient role model to follow. Kirk Douglas had played unimportant supporting roles as 'nice' people until he took the role of a ruthless, obsessed gangster in the 1947 film, *Build My Gallows High*. That part allowed him to display an unsuspected range and he was elevated up the pecking order in Hollywood as a direct result. Thanks to the role as the 'nasty' Gordon Gekko forty years later his son was able to make the same quantum leap in prestige and power.

Gekko's famous 'Greed is Good' speech, a nine-minute hymn to rampant materialism, came to represent the ethos of the film and the age. The words spoken by Douglas were an eerie echo of a real speech by Ivan F. Boesky, since barred forever from trading in the United States Securities industry. The speech by Boesky began, 'The point is, ladies and gentlemen, greed is good. Greed works, greed is right . . .'

Many viewers failed to notice the simple morality fable behind the power dressing. Faust returned, sponsored by Gucci and Armani, and took up a corporate post seeking gold and fame and power. In an utterly mesmeric performance Douglas as Gordon Gekko became a modern Mephistopheles luring and corrupting and entrapping the gullible Charlie Sheen. It was an intensely captivating *tour de force* and gave even more strength to the arguments of those who had always believed that Michael Douglas was a very fine actor indeed.

In the perception of many people in the industry Michael Douglas was a producer and sometime actor. The extent of his abilities had come to general recognition first in *Romancing*; then *Fatal Attraction* and *Wall Street* strengthened his reputation. 'You must remember that prior to the *Fatal Attraction/Wall Street* era I wasn't getting that much respect as an actor. And people often resent you if you're second generation. And if you're a producer, which I was primarily, they connect it with being a businessman all the time. They find it distasteful!'

There is also the not inconsiderable question of jealousy for Michael Douglas obviously created resentment in some quarters because he had made acting and producing equally successful.

It was *Wall Street* which really established him as a major player. And it wasn't coincidence that such elevation came on the first occasion he was encouraged to play a real bastard.

It was Kirk who recognized a latent quality in Michael, a quality which surfaced to surprising effect in *Wall Street*. As he admitted, 'My father has always said, "You're gonna do a great killer sometime. You're such a charming guy, but they're gonna find out the prick you really are!" '

Douglas thought long and hard about how to play Gekko. 'You take essences. In some you pick up the seduction and the charm. In some you pick up the intellect. In some the killer instinct – you can see it in the eyes. I never saw Gekko as a bully – he didn't need to be. The ones I know in really powerful positions can afford to seem humble.'

Coming off the back of *Fatal Attraction* the impact of *Wall Street* catapulted Michael Douglas to superstardom. It was another film which became an element of public debate focusing people's attention on issues rather than personalities. Some critics objected that the characters presented in the film are occasionally little more than two-dimensional caricatures. If true that was a weakness in the writing which was the responsibility of Stanley Weisner and director Oliver Stone. The actors, Douglas, Charlie and Martin Sheen *et al*, could only make the most of the screenplay they were given, and invariably the performances are polished and intense. Martin Sheen's role was especially transparent and called for little from such an accomplished actor. His son brought a nervous desperation to his role which was quite convincing, but it was Gekko's picture.

Oliver Stone commented fiercely on what Douglas brought to the film.

> He was a little lazy, he came to the picture with a bit of a Hollywood attitude, and I don't work that way. I work fast, no re-shooting, not much margin for error. He didn't cotton on to that school of making pictures so we had some problems and I got tough with him. I think I brought out the angry side of him. I wanted a kid of Kirk Douglas in this movie. 'Where the hell's your father? You're a wimp! You're a Mister Nice Guy!' Then he got on top of it quick, hot, and he was good.

For his part Douglas reacted badly to some of Stone's more idiosyncratic methods. On-set reports detailed a number of aggressive confrontations between director and star. Stone's declared policy of antagonizing Douglas into a major performance realized its objectives, but caused great blow-ups during filming. 'Oliver doesn't coddle his actors,' admitted Douglas. 'If he was a grunt in Vietnam he's certainly a commander in moviemaking.'

A mutual respect developed between director and star, fuelled by a growing appreciation of the other's abilities, especially as misconceptions were dispelled. 'I was warned by everyone in Hollywood,' admitted Stone cagily, 'that Michael couldn't act, that he was a producer more than an actor, and would spend all his time in his trailer on the phone.'

Eventually even the obsessive Oliver Stone would concede of Douglas that 'when he's acting he gives it his all!'

That level of commitment generally surprised people. Even those like Stone who met Michael Douglas expecting him to be a dilettante playboy were invariably shocked by his genuine professionalism. It is difficult now to understand just what Stone and the others were expecting in Douglas.

The director also grew to be impressed by the way Douglas accepted the challenge posed by the part. Stone had studied Douglas in *Romancing the Stone* and discovered in the actor's cavalier performance 'an edge which I found interesting'. He had only met Douglas on a couple of informal social occasions prior to *Wall Street*. For the part he was seeking an actor with some business knowledge and experience, and the wide immersion of

147

Douglas in production made him ideally suited to Stone.

And yet despite his choice of Douglas for the role the process of filming was often terribly stormy. Stone chose Michael Douglas because of something latent within the actor but it was a process of conflict which would bring that hidden quality to the surface. 'I thought his acting was soft and formulaic and I came down on him,' commented Stone. 'We were using a lot of hand-held cameras a few inches from his face, and there were long speeches. I don't think he had ever worked with anyone like me before. Michael has to be pushed sometimes; he can get lazy!'

Whilst conceding the extent of his debt to the director Michael Douglas, as ever, is careful in his choice of words on Oliver Stone. The politician doesn't badmouth someone who could later prove to be friend or ally, and Douglas has long since developed that self-interested caution. 'Oliver and I had not a lot of fun on *Wall Street*,' he admitted. 'And I've come to realize in hindsight that he had his own reasons for what he wanted to get out of me as an actor.'

His various involvements in producing enabled Douglas to draw an interesting comparison between Gordon Gekko and himself.

> The other thing I drew from my produciary background is that revenge is wonderful. Gekko thrives on the energy of anybody who's ever

crossed him. He cherishes holding grudges. It gives him the fuel to keep going. I know that during all the years when I dealt with rejection on film projects, it was an emotion that, directed in a positive way, gave me the endurance and stamina that I needed to get a picture made. Or in Gordon's case to get deals done.

Oliver Stone clearly recognized something of this taut viciousness in Douglas. 'The most interesting thing in casting is to find an actor when he is about to change, to get him at the point when he's going to make a change in his personality,' commented Stone to CBS Television. 'Michael Douglas had never been tough before *Wall Street*. I think that's what's exciting about directing actors, to find something new in them.'

Douglas certainly worked hard to prepare adequately for the role, putting more physical work into preparation than for any film since *Running*. He lost weight and developed a sleek hardness which perfectly fitted Gekko's viciously smooth persona. 'Creating a character is sometimes a lot easier than playing yourself. *Fatal*, for instance, was the exact opposite – dealing with a situation moment by moment as you might, getting as close to yourself as possible.'

He did a lot of work around corporate establishments in New York, studying the accounts of the activities of such corporate predators as Carl Icahn and T. Boone Pickens. As a basis for work he also drew comparisons with other real-live characters like Ivan Boesky.

It is a lasting tribute to the performance delivered by Michael Douglas that the name Gekko passed so rapidly into public usage. When people are looking for a single word to summarize the selfish, rapacious eighties they often turn to 'Gekko'. The use of a single name to represent a whole era epitomizes the stunning impact of the film.

That success received its ultimate recognition on 11 April 1988 when Michael Douglas took the award as Best Actor at the Oscar ceremony.

It was a bitter-sweet presentation. To many people's surprise *Wall Street* didn't take any other awards so the recognition of his work in the film was even stronger. Diandra attended the ceremony, inevitably and quite naturally. Kirk didn't, preferring to wait at home and watch on television. Father and son met later that evening, after the ceremony, when Kirk hosted a lavish celebration party. The moment of meeting was extremely poignant with the son clutching the one golden prize which had evaded the father during a forty-year career.

All those great films, including classics like *Lust for Life*, *Lonely are the Brave* and *Champion*, and no Oscar. And then the son comes in holding that precious little gold statuette!

It must have been a moment of extremely mixed emotions for Kirk, pride and disappointment in an emotional smorgasbord which would be hard for most people to understand. Yet his joy at Michael's success was undiluted and clearly genuine, as was his pride at the work Michael produced for the film. 'My father paid me the greatest compliment. He said, "Son, I noticed the resemblance between us but, five minutes into the picture, I forgot you were my son. I forgot everything. You really nailed that part!" '

Michael's speech of thanks at the ceremony was simple and touching. He introduced his remarks by talking about the role 'not many people thought I could play'. The main body of his acceptance speech involved thanks to the people who had been most instrumental in his career and life, and inevitably they were family members.

'I'd like to dedicate this award to my parents and step-parents, who have been supportive over the years, and particularly to my father, who I don't think ever missed one of my college productions, for his continued support, and in particular for helping his son step out of his shadow. I'll be eternally grateful to you, Dad.'

He went on a little longer but that delicate dedication to his father caused a suppressed sob of emotion in many throats at the ceremony. It was odd to see the number of people who freely admitted to loathing Kirk Douglas vigorously applauding such a tribute to him from his son.

Many personalities find difficulty in coming

151

down from the kind of mammoth success represented by the Oscar. Perhaps wisely Michael Douglas intended to take a step back after the award. He had learned bitter lessons from the kind of punishing schedule maintained by his father over previous decades. 'I'd like to learn from the mistakes my father made – three pictures a year and never stopping.'

He had also completed his appointed schedule of two films virtually back-to-back and so felt perfectly entitled to indulge himself with a prolonged spell away from the camera.

Yet the demands made by the film industry are insatiable, especially for a hot commodity like an Oscar winner. He ruefully realized the differences which that tiny statuette made. 'My acting life has totally changed. I'm the flavour of the month, or whatever it is.'

More succinctly he remarked, in relation to the Oscar award, 'It's all gravy now!'

Despite his declared intention to step back from acting and producing he was back before the camera within six months. He replied to barbed remarks about his lack of resolve by glibly repeating his cheeky line from *Romancing*, 'I ain't cheap – but I can be had!'

Such a mercenary attitude may divulge his true feelings about his next projects. For the first film after the Oscar award the location was Japan, in a thriller, *Black Rain*, directed by Ridley Scott. Once again the team of Sherry Lansing and Stanley

Jaffe were producers, although the film credits include the line 'in association with Michael Douglas'. Such an arrangement meant that he was involved in production decisions without carrying all the burden himself.

'In the case of *Black Rain* Sherry and Stanley would come to me and suggest a drink at the end of the day to talk over production matters. Whereas before I'd be involved in implementation this time it was just advice.'

This arrangement seemed to offer an ideal alternative to the high-pressure total involvement which was his lot on films like *Romancing* and *The China Syndrome*. The new association took some weight off his shoulders and saved him from the strain which afflicted him on earlier productions.

Sherry Lansing was enthusiastic about the film. 'I've got a hot, sexy action movie with substance, and I think Michael is a huge star.'

The film was something of a departure for Douglas in that he played a very physical role, well away from the urbanity of Dan Gallagher and even Gordon Gekko. New York homicide detective Nick Conklin is a rough, nasty corrupt policeman driven by emotional pressures he cannot comprehend. The meat of the film is the clash of cultures as represented in the conflict between Conklin and the Tokyo detective played by Ken Takakura. Michael Douglas produced a gritty, snarling performance which added another facet to his growing reputation as an accomplished actor.

It was obviously a surprise to many people that Douglas was actually such a competent actor but his canon of film work, especially through *Romancing*, *Fatal Attraction* and *Wall Street*, had demonstrated his capabilities.

Black Rain bolstered that reputation but was not a major success as a film. In many respects it was too dark, too grim, for public taste. The imposition of a New York style cop film on a Japanese background was an interesting, even brave experiment, typical of Ridley Scott, but it didn't really work. At times Douglas seemed uncomfortable in his work, and whilst this reinforced the element of alienation it registered on the audience that this was not one of Michael Douglas' happiest experiences.

He enjoyed his immersion in the character of Nick Conklin. 'It's nice to worry about having to be a diplomat while in character. I was accused of doing too many "nice" pictures earlier in my career. But the role was a little unrelenting. He's a dark son of a bitch – a guy who's lost faith and is living on the edge. He's begun to be destructive.'

Some of the complexities of plot imposed by Ridley Scott were confusing. In the end the film seemed to depend too much on the strength of the confrontation between the characters of Michael Douglas and Ken Takakura. The various machinations involving the Japanese underworld bewildered many people and the film was unfortunate enough to hit America at a time when the anti-Japanese sentiment was reaching its peak.

Many reviewers found the change of character for Michael Douglas too abrupt for comfort. The urbane, sophisticated Manhattan man, as personified by Dan Gallagher or Gordon Gekko, had become Nick Conklin, a violent, racist, corrupt street-fighter, who was more suited to the ghettos of Harlem than the opulence of Fifth Avenue.

He was then committed to starting work on his next film with hardly any respite.

That year was real hard on my family. I left in the middle of September for Japan and shot well into 1989 and then went into *War of the Roses* with a five-day break. I finished *Roses* in July. That makes ten months. *Rain* was in Japan. *Roses* was in Los Angeles. We were living in New York. There's no way you can balance your personal life when you're in every single scene of a picture and working sixteen hours a day.

Wall Street had been shot entirely in New York taking Douglas back to the comfortable days of *Chorus Line* when he could stay at home and travel to work each morning like any other multi-millionaire commuter.

Black Rain took him away from home into Asia. *War of the Roses* took him back to California for a prolonged spell. Diandra and Cameron were able to fly out to be with him, and he took advantage of breaks in filming to get back to New York. Nevertheless the extended separation put further strains on a marriage which once again began to provide fertile pickings for the gossip columnists.

Such sympathetic writers totally ignored the frequent announcements from Douglas that he had embarked on a policy of completing two films back-to-back and then taking one or two years off. In 1988/9 he filmed first *Black Rain* then *War of the Roses* before commencing an eighteen-month sabbatical. He then worked on first *Shining Through* and then *Basic Instinct* before again starting a prolonged vacation.

Sadly the gossip columnists disregarded the evidence of their own eyes and implied that his sustained bouts of filming were proof of continuing problems with the marriage. It didn't matter how often the couple protested that they were happy, the gossips thrived on acrimony not harmony.

In those circumstances it was a most unfortunate coincidence that the subject matter of *Roses* was a very acrimonious divorce. Several acerbic columnists tried unsuccessfully to link the marriage and the film, but Douglas ignored their remarks and spoke only about the film. 'It's about how people who love each other that much can end up hating each other with the same degree of passion. Yes, it's sick – but hopefully good sick!'

Played as a black comedy the film brought together the three stars of *Romancing* and *Jewel*.

The film also used the services of many crew members who had worked on the earlier films, and this was an element which Douglas obviously enjoyed. 'It's family. Moviemaking is always a delicate balance of egos and diplomacy. But we all knew each other on *Roses* and we've developed a shorthand by now. There's no room for egos. Nobody buys it!'

All three senior members of the cast were at pains to insist that *War of the Roses* was not the third part of the trilogy. 'It's not *Romancing the Stone Part Three*,' insisted Douglas. 'That was our only concern when Kathleen came on board.'

Despite his denials there were still critics who saw the inclusion of Kathleen Turner as signifying nothing but a sequel. Understandably Douglas had a different view. 'She was chosen because she's so good and because it's a dark comedy. There may be other people who are more comedic, but she keeps it grounded in reality.'

Once again the character played by Michael Douglas does unpleasant, sometimes repulsive things, but his roguish charm proves captivating and he never totally loses our sympathy. A three film spread like *Romancing*, *Jewel* and *War of the Roses* gives the leading players a special chance to know each other's work. Kathleen Turner had had an unrivalled chance to gauge the development of Douglas as an actor over a period of years, and she declared herself deeply impressed by his single-minded approach to performing some of the less delicate acts like urinating in the fish tureen. 'A lot of actors would sort of give a wink to the camera over their shoulder, just to let the audience know "I'm not really like this". I never saw Michael do that!'

The film proved to be a modest success, and that, added to the unenthusiastic reception for *Black Rain*, represented another temporary blip in the spiralling career of Michael Douglas. He was rather unfortunate in that people compared the massive success of *Fatal Attraction* and *Wall Street* with the comparatively unsuccessful *Roses* and *Black Rain*. In that respect he could reflect ruefully on the comparative costs of success.

In another arm of the entertainment industry, recording an album which goes on to sell ten million copies would represent, for most artists, a monumental success. For someone like Michael Jackson sales on that level would mean a distinct disappointment. Michael Douglas found himself in the same ironic situation with *Black Rain* and *War of the Roses*. Nothing could have matched the incredible impact of *Wall Street* and *Fatal Attraction* and yet, for the two later films, there was a clear perception of failure.

After the less than ecstatic reviews it was no wonder that he retreated again into some quiet avenue of semi-retirement. Licking his wounds after the excesses of *Black Rain* and *War of the Roses* he opted for another withdrawal. 'I'm going to take a year off as an actor because I really don't know what to do now. I'm tired and I'm sort of dry. I feel I've run the gamut of roles.'

This was a period of introspection for Douglas. He was intent on taking time in Santa Barbara and particularly in the pretty villa in Majorca to look at his career and life and see where it was going. He had become a powerful force in the industry, and totally lost any automatic connection with Kirk in people's minds. When he started in the business that would have been one of his greatest ambitions.

During that lengthy period off the screen he concentrated on building up his production interests and also on cementing family ties. The bonds with Diandra and Cameron had inevitably become slightly frayed, mainly because of the lengthy spells he had been forced to spend away from home working on location on the two most recent films. This did not mean that the marriage was under threat; far from it, but he sensibly devoted himself almost entirely to wife and son during the regular sabbaticals.

Another period as house-husband recharged emotional and creative batteries and left him able to lounge around and indulge in his favourite activity of watching sports. He took great delight in being able to sit around like any ordinary American male watching football or baseball on television, proving yet again what a hold sport has on him.

'And sports, all the sports – I've got great sports stations on cable. They play sports around the clock. I love watching sports. I love anything where I don't know what the ending's going to be.'

Once that prolonged sabbatical had ended he went into his next picture, *Shining Through* with Melanie Griffith. Based on the novel by Susan Isaacs this World War Two story of espionage and intrigue was filmed in England and on location in Germany and Austria during 1991. The film reunited Douglas with many of the crew members who had worked with him on *Romancing* and *Jewel*. Once again there was no involvement on the production side for Michael Douglas. This was a simple acting job demanding nothing more substantial than his brooding presence and dynamic counterpoint to the simpering sensuality of Melanie Griffith.

He had actively pursued the role of Ed Leland, lawyer and secret spy, realizing that in the role he could achieve something of a change of direction. 'After *Fatal Attraction* and *War of the Roses* I was looking to do something more heroic and idealistic,' he admitted. '*Shining Through* offered me the chance to play a period part and a romantic lead, plus the chance to work with Melanie Griffith.'

Just as with Oliver Stone and *Wall Street* the director of *Shining Through*, David Seltzer, actually wanted Michael Douglas for the role. 'Leland is strong, inaccessible, self-centred and quick-tempered – all those things that no woman would admit to wanting in a partner today, but which made for a very sexy, appealing man in the 1940s.'

In that respect Michael Douglas proved ideal for the role. 'He has a darker side,' admitted Seltzer. 'He's a real guy, very romantic and strong, and that's what this part needed.' Commenting on the strengths of the film Seltzer added, 'He's macho, and I hope that kind of macho is coming back. Michael stands up in a way that Gary Cooper did!'

He looked remarkably like Kirk in certain scenes, and it proved very difficult when watching the film to ignore the comparison, particularly in the final frames when he was made up to look like an old man, about the same age as his father was in real life.

The film was no more than a moderate success. The gaping weaknesses in the plot proved more memorable than its high points. It wasn't helped by reported remarks like that from Melanie Griffith who, reacting to her extensive research prior to the film, commented, 'I didn't know that six million Jews were killed. That's a lot of people!'

Most reviewers had a wonderful time concentrating on the holes and implausibilities in the plot. Many people commented on the glaring similarities between the role of Melanie Griffith in *Working Girl* and her later role in *Shining Through*.

Unfortunately the latter film failed to capture the joy and excitement of the Oscar-winning *Working Girl*.

Scenes in *Shining Through* like the inverted tribute to *Casablanca* in which Douglas boarded the plane on the misty runway leaving the girl behind really didn't help the film. Sadly, *Shining Through* was another ill-chosen project which did little to elevate the reputation of Michael Douglas. Once again he found himself male lead in a film where the female lead took prominence. It was a film in which Melanie Griffith shone and, powerful though his performance was, he was clearly playing second fiddle to her. It was undeniably her film, and the look of faint embarrassment appearing on his face spoke volumes about what he thought of the film.

He had been searching for a heroic part and saw that potential in *Shining Through*. He was now at a stage where he could choose roles to suit his mood or, more particularly, provide another facet to his canon of work. His next role would achieve the latter objective to an unprecedented extent.

8 Commercial Instincts

Greater hopes were pinned on *Basic Instinct* which the publicists busily promoted as the 'erotic thriller for the nineties'. Closed-set shooting was intended to restrict information about the film prior to its release but it was clearly aimed at the same territory as *Fatal Attraction*. It quickly attracted the snappy description as a Cops 'n' Copulation thriller, and the sexy, steamy scenes presented problems in giving the film a rating in the States.

'I saw it as a sexy, psychological thriller, a sort of *Fatal Attraction* for the nineties,' admitted Douglas. 'It resembles the kind of detective novel you might read in the privacy of your own bedroom. Not really smutty but certainly stimulating!'

He admitted that there were several reasons for his choosing to take the part but was honest enough to concede that vanity was one of the elements behind his decision. 'After *Shining Through* I wanted to do something sexy. I'd always seen these lists of the year's ten sexiest actors and I never saw my name on any of them. I felt like I was chopped liver, a character actor. But when I looked back at my career, I said, "Well, what do you want, man? You've always played character roles"!'

Even during the course of filming *Basic Instinct* managed to create a furore which led to pickets and threats of action against cinemas showing the film. This movement was led by an unlikely coalition of gay protest groups angered by the plotline of the film.

On the surface *Basic Instinct* was a convoluted thriller resurrecting a plot which has served Hollywood well over the years, most recently in Al Pacino's *Sea of Love*. A San Francisco detective investigates a crime, the murder of an elderly rock star, and in the process falls in love with a suspect in the case. That suspect, writer Catherine Tramell, sleeps with the real-life models for her characters male and female. Her books feature graphic descriptions of various murders and those savage homicides have a nasty habit of actually happening.

The female star of the film, Sharon Stone, was sure of its likely appeal. 'This isn't a movie that's meant to make everyone feel great. It's a movie that's meant to make you feel great and wonderful and disturbed and awful and happy and angry and "I'm not gonna go" and then you're the first one at the theatre because you want to see what it's all about. It's that kind of movie. It's sensationalistic!'

The different element in *Basic Instinct* is that the detective, Michael Douglas, is pursuing a serial killer who is portrayed in the film as a female bisexual. Her particular *modus operandi* is to seduce and tie men up and then kill them with an ice pick, and it was this exclusive choice of target which attracted attention and fury.

The homosexual community in America is a very voluble minority and it quickly picked up on the alleged sexual stereotyping involved in *Basic Instinct*. Lobbying began, particularly from the executive director of GLAAD, Ellen Carlton, and writer Joe Eszterhas, a local resident north of San Francisco, was forced into a number of uncomfortable compromises. At one point he offered to give main character Michael Douglas a new line of dialogue stating that the best people he had met in the city were gay.

There was also the intention to run a disclaimer at the beginning of the film asserting that the film was not a reflection of the behaviour patterns of all lesbians and bisexuals. Although the disclaimer idea was stillborn it came as a direct result of the protests of groups like NOW, the National Organization for Women claiming the film was, 'one of the most blatantly misogynistic films in recent memory'. Judy Sisneros, spokesperson for Queer Nation, also complained that *Basic Instinct* added to 'the overwhelmingly negative portrayal of gays and lesbians in movies, with its psychological profiles of lesbians and bi women as evil, diabolical'.

The efforts of Eszterhas to distance himself from the backlash were not entirely successful. He wasn't the most popular man in Hollywood before this crisis. He had written hits like *Jagged Edge*, *Flashdance* and *Music Box*, but became famous or infamous because of a bitter dispute between himself and Michael Ovitz.

Independent production company Carolco paid Eszterhas a record $3 million for the screenplay of *Basic Instinct* in the summer of 1990 and thereby created a wave of resentment and jealousy against him.

A constant theme in his earlier works was psychological manipulation and in Catherine Tramell's character Eszterhas created a master of contrivance and intrigue. 'The film is a gigantic mind game that extends into the bedroom,' commented Eszterhas, adding that it was a 'strange and twisted love story about homicidal impulse!'

His various later pontifications on the film industry did little to endear him to the film community, and there were few who pitied Eszterhas for the controversy in which he had become embroiled.

He then confirmed many people's darker fears by wriggling out of the controversy and quite skilfully leaving the film's star, Michael Douglas, and its producers to face the fury of the protesters. Even the mild-mannered, and usually politic, Douglas was forced to voice his anger at Eszterhas. 'Look, it's a hot, sexy thriller. That's why I wanted to do it. Joe claimed it was a matter of principle, and we now know this man has no principles.'

The threats from the protesters were hardly mild and could not be taken lightly. One unfortunate chap, owner of Rawhide 11, a gay and lesbian country and western bar in San Francisco, allowed some filming to take place in his bar. Death threats were spray-painted on the walls of his bar one evening, his Mercedes car was badly vandalized, and he has been in fear of violence or death ever since. This despite the fact that he is a member of the community himself.

The lobby against the film was powerful and articulate. Various unlikely script changes were demanded including making the character played by Douglas into a homosexual, which, on the face of it, would have destroyed one of the main elements in the film. The lobby also required major changes to the script which would have further changed the emphasis of the film. The protesters demanded that the serial killer should be seen to attack both men and women. This would have reduced the perceived impact of the killer's actions so that she would not be seen as a man-hater.

All the entreaties for such changes were made

to Eszterhas. He argued openly with Verhoeven over changes which the director requested. Such requested changes involved more explicit lesbian scenes and reputedly the desire by Verhoeven to be the first mainstream director to show the erect male sex organ in a Hollywood film.

The first script meeting, in October 1990, involving Verhoeven, Eszterhas, Michael Douglas and putative producer Erwin Winkler developed into an extremely acrimonious exchange. Verhoeven initially wanted Eszterhas to alter the direction of his original script and add various bisexual and lesbian scenes to the mainly heterosexual scenes presented by Eszterhas. Not unreasonably the writer resented such salacious interference and this conflict started the fires which were to smoulder and flare up throughout filming.

Because Eszterhas refused to co-operate with Verhoeven the director engaged another writer to structure the script closer to his vision. Gary Goldman, writer of *Total Recall*, came in with Verhoeven to produce the updated script which would include more of the elements which left Verhoeven salivating at the prospect.

In *Basic Instinct* the lesbian relationship between Sharon Stone and her screen lover Roxy, played by Leilani Sarelli, is sketched in by the pair kissing passionately. It is said that the wife of Joe Eszterhas claims that such scenes spring from the murky depths of his own sexual fantasies. Even should that be true it is undeniable that Verhoeven portrays that lesbian romance as the most honest relationship in the film. 'That's the only real love, probably, because all the others are kind of weird!'

The film reveals that Roxy had killed members of her family in the past; Catherine is seen in a relationship with another woman who was also responsible for another mass murder. Even the third major female character, Beth Gardner, has a lesbian past and there is a suspicion of blood on her hands. In many ways the protesters missed the key point namely that the film is an attack and slur on women generally. The developed script became a lurid catalogue of male fantasies and more than a few reviewers commented on the degrading view of women presented in Verhoeven's masterpiece.

'I think *Basic Instinct* really does portray these women in a very negative way,' commented Sharon Stone. 'But I also think that every story has an antagonist and protagonist and there's only two genders to pick from!'

Intended producer Irwin Winkler was a personal friend of Eszterhas and by December 1990 both writer and proposed producer announced that they were distancing themselves from the project. A fresh producer, Allan Marshall, came in, and Verhoeven began pre-production work while waiting for Goldman to deliver the new script. After several months he realized that only the original script presented by Eszterhas would work and he had the good grace to admit the fact in public. Verhoeven admitted:

The lesbian scene never worked. It was just stupid, so we simply changed a few lines to make Michael's character stronger and we sent it over to Joe and he loved the script. We all made up in the papers to show everybody that it was just a big misunderstanding and it was. I mean, it was really wrong, and I have acknowledged throughout the year that my proposal was really stupid and childlike, and I have no problem repeating that now!

The principals, writer, director, star and new producer, met for meetings to enable the film to move forward. In the fresh spirit of conciliation those meetings should have inaugurated a period of co-operation but instead they threw up the thorniest dispute of all. Michael Douglas recalled:

At kiss-and-make-up time we began to hear rumours about the gay activist attacks we were going to face. I clearly remember saying to Joe, 'Look, this is brewing. Do you have a problem with it?' and he said, 'No. I believe, in every group there's deviant behaviour.' Then, a second time, when we were in rehearsal in San Francisco, I asked him the same question and he said, 'No, absolutely not' – he didn't have a problem. And I said, 'Good, because we may need your support – you're from the Bay Area.'

More meetings were arranged but they now incorporated the protesters. The same principals were involved meeting with a delegation from the various protest groups who were just starting to get organized. The principals agreed on a policy for the critical meeting in June 1991 but as soon as it opened Eszterhas reneged on that understanding.

'The problem that occurred later was, of course, when Joe suddenly wanted to change the script because of the attacks of the gay community,' stated Verhoeven grimly.

In a markedly sanctimonious speech and a chilling reminder of the House on Unamerican Activities hearings of the fifties Eszterhas abandoned his friends and joined the opposition. He condemned the film-makers, the movie community, and declared a willingness to make changes to please the protesters.

He announced that he was working on a revised script which would have changed the character played by Michael Douglas into a lesbian, and had the bisexual killer attacking women as well as men. There was even thought given to the actress to play the newly castrated lead in the film and Kathleen Turner was heavily promoted. Fortunately for all concerned the idea came to nothing.

'Joe stabbed Allan Marshall in the back,' stated Douglas bitterly. 'I can understand that he was nervous about what the activists might do to his wife and kids, but he should have called Allan and told him in advance, instead of just blurting it out in the meeting.'

Eszterhas dignified the rabid demands by considering them, and thereby lost the respect of Carolco and Douglas. The ultimate act of artistic abandonment came when Eszterhas publicly disowned his original script and took the side of the gays and lesbians in San Francisco who had been trying to disrupt filming. A continuing stream of bitter quotes from Michael Douglas and Paul Verhoeven show that they felt artistically betrayed by the actions of the writer.

It was an unusual controversy as it was prompted by a script rather than a completed film. The fact that protesters were so well-informed about the storyline before cameramen started work meant that the protesters were able to get organized before location shooting began. Immediate disruption took the form of packs of people following location shooting and making as much noise as possible. Whistles were blown, gongs banged, and general bedlam was the result. The leader of one of the protest groups defined their disruptive tactics as, 'We're blowing our whistles to let the world know we need help!'

The problems became so acute that on some occasions at least fifty members of the riot police division of the San Francisco Police Department were on hand to keep order.

Carolco, the production company responsible

for *Basic Instinct* in conjunction with TriStar, was angry about the disruption and even more explicit about the perceived treachery of Eszterhas. 'I consider his changes patronizing drivel,' snarled Peter Hoffman, Carolco's chief executive. 'Joe Eszterhas is a snivelling hypocrite and I have no use for him. Besides we would never change a script in response to political pressure.'

Carolco had difficulties of its own being some $200 million in debt even before the film opened. *Basic Instinct* cost almost $50 million and, although a good return is virtually guaranteed, the ongoing controversy is not likely to help the struggling production company. Many people within the industry are suspicious of the practices of such companies as Carolco blaming them for the fantastic spiral in fees during the eighties. One of the company's earlier financial coups was to give Arnold Schwarzenegger $10 million as a basic fee plus 15 per cent of the gross of *Total Recall*. Few tears were shed at the sight of Carolco caught up in the expensive controversy of *Basic Instinct*.

However, the deluge of publicity is certain to drag even more people into the cinemas curious, as ever, to see what is causing such a fuss. Carolco will ultimately benefit from the problems which beset the film before it was even completed.

The man slated as original producer, Irwin Winkler, another industry veteran, didn't even make it to the commencement of filming. He resigned in the wake of the Eszterhas furore, taking his agreed $1 million fee with him and stating bitterly that the director was obsessed with showing people's bodies 'in various states of excitement'. The director was Paul Verhoeven, the Dutchman who had come to fame via such deep character studies as *Total Recall* and *RoboCop*. One critic said of *Basic Instinct* that in it Verhoeven 'did for sex what he earlier did for violence in *Total Recall* and *RoboCop*'!

Earlier in his career, back in Europe he had also achieved a certain notoriety through films like *The Fourth Man* which dealt with various themes including bisexuality and homosexuality. Hollywood first became aware of the Dutchman when his film, *Turkish Delight*, was nominated for the Best Foreign Language Film Oscar in 1973, but it was near the $300 million taken by *Total Recall* which made him an attractive proposition for TriStar.

Verhoeven was clearly impressed by his work on the film despite the misgivings voiced by many people. 'I feel I really succeeded in making a Hitchcock for the nineties, more sexual, a bit more evil, more provocative probably than Hitchcock would ever do, but he was limited by the period he was living in where everything was a little more puritan, and I thought he would have loved this movie!'

A close observer of the film world commented

that 'The film, *Basic Instinct*, is a clumsy mixture of Adrian Lyne's films, *Fatal Attraction* and *9½ Weeks*, without being as good or as honest as either of them!'

The sexual boundaries mapped out by earlier films like *9½ Weeks* were further extended by *Basic Instinct*. Sharon Stone admitted, 'Michael Douglas and I went as far as anyone could go – so far, in fact, that I don't know how they'll ever get a rating!' The stark explicitness of scenes coupling Douglas with Sharon Stone or Jeanne Tripplehorn were such that the film had difficulty obtaining a rating in America, but that was certainly part of Verhoeven's master plan. He had the dream of producing a film which would push back the boundaries but even so he shot several scenes from a variety of angles with the express purpose of having stronger and weaker versions of the same scenes.

'In certain cases, like the shot where he's between her legs we were laughing because we knew even while we were shooting it that we would never get away with that in the American market!' admitted Verhoeven.

Such voyeuristic pleasure was at odds with some of Stone's pronouncements. 'I'm a trained actor and serious about what I'm doing, and although the movie is sensationalistic, my acting isn't!'

Cut after cut of the film was delivered, each subsequent version slightly more watered down

175

in a calculated attempt to reach a print which would result in an acceptable rating without emasculating Verhoeven's film. Big money and big commercial interests were involved. The original cut rated the film NC-17, a relatively new rating created by MPAA just to accommodate the problems created by the sexually explicit film *Henry and June*. Yet all parties recognized that such a rating would be commercial suicide for *Basic Instinct*.

An 'R' rating was the desired status for the film particularly as relatively few cinemas in America will show an NC-17 film. The problems created by an NC-17 rating even extend to promotion as a number of television and radio stations plus many newspapers will not carry advertising for such films.

Video is assuming ever greater importance as part of the overall marketing plan for a major film. One of the most important companies marketing videos after the cinema release of a film is Blockbuster Video and their declared policy is not to touch NC-17 rated films. Blockbuster controls almost fifteen per cent of the total market and it would be commercially suicidal for any film company to fail to utilize Blockbuster's marketing power by voluntarily accepting an NC-17 rating.

Both the Sony Corporation offshoot TriStar and Carolco, the two companies involved in the production of *Basic Instinct*, are strictly commercial organizations to which the production of an

NC-17 film would be anathema. 'It had to be an R,' stated the legendary Mike Medavoy, head of TriStar. 'The risk is too big!'

Verhoeven's contract stipulated that he had to deliver a film which would receive an R rating. Because he had shot several of the most contentious scenes in a milder and a more explicit form he was able to release both an American version with an R rating and an overseas version which would be truer to his initial concept. Some critics accused Verhoeven of cynical exploitation of his cast, but this was not the only time Verhoeven encountered this objection.

Both *Total Recall* and *RoboCop* had ranged the MPAA against him, and he had suffered the agonies of trimming his original cut to obtain the necessary MPAA rating. Verhoeven described himself as the expert on how to prepare a controversial film for MPAA inspection. He was expecting to meet that problem with *Basic Instinct* as was Michael Douglas. Both director and star were fully conscious of the need to deliver a film which wouldn't receive the prohibitive NC-17 rating, which in America is tantamount to pornography, but both were fiercely protective of the film. Douglas admitted before the release of the film:

The only controversy I foresee is with the American rating system. Most US distributors won't touch the European version because so many movie theatres are in malls, which attract kids and families. We're fighting for an 'adult' label like they have in Britain because I think adults have a right to see the film we made. It's kind of hush-hush right now because you don't want your US audience to know there's this other, sexier picture out there that they're not going to see!

'I have made a cut that I can still defend,' Verhoeven stated, 'but I don't know if there is much to go beyond that.' Douglas, whilst sharing his director's sentiments, expressed his feelings in a much earthier, Western-film manner. 'We're going to be watching out for the picture!'

Following the lopping away of forty-two seconds from the delivered print the MPAA accepted *Basic Instinct* and, to the great satisfaction of all parties concerned, the film received its critical R rating in mid-February 1992 just weeks before the American cinemas received first prints of the film.

It had been a bruising process for Michael Douglas. Besides the difficulties caused by the protesters, and the gruelling demands of the love scenes, he also encountered problems with his director. Verhoeven has a very precise, personal way of working. Very unusually among top directors he likes to storyboard the whole film and adhere strictly to it, ruling out the more normal improvisation or collaboration between actors and director. Many actors and actresses find this constricting.

Michael Douglas was more affected by the absence of interaction between himself and the director. 'Paul never told me how I was doing – he never said a word,' admitted Douglas. 'So that was hard for me. I don't go to dailies and he just never talks!'

His experience as star in major films enabled him to draw an interesting comparison between Verhoeven and Oliver Stone after working with both.

'Playing Nick was a very painful process for me because Paul didn't talk to me much about my character. I think that maybe there was a purpose to this. Oliver stone used the same technique on me in *Wall Street*. When you're appearing in every scene, you start getting crazy, which is probably, I realized in hindsight, what Paul wanted.'

This lack of contact led to a famous incident culminating in an animated discussion between the pair in the trailer used by Douglas on the set. What actually happened, and what was truly said, has remained cloaked in secrecy but one immediate result of the meeting was that Verhoeven was rushed to hospital and kept in for several days with what was described as a severe nosebleed.

The resulting medical bulletin blamed the illness on a combination of stress caused by filming and an old childhood ailment. Some members of the crew could be seen surreptitiously gazing at the knuckles on the right hand of Michael Douglas while Verhoeven was away.

Paul Verhoeven was, and is, a very strong, single-minded individual. Despite the many accusations of sexual obsession and exploitation made against him Verhoeven remains convinced that the film carries an important central truth. 'The film is a tale about the seduction of evil and the charming face evil wears,' he maintained. 'It's difficult to discern between real evil and charm.'

It was impossible for any of those intimately involved with the film to remain aloof from the mounting controversy. Although he was not personally attacked by the protesters in the same way as Douglas or certain others Paul Verhoeven was compelled to consider the wider implications of *Basic Instinct*.

'I don't think that homosexuality or bisexuality should be made an issue in this film. If anything I hope people come out of this movie feeling that any sexual orientation is natural.'

Verhoeven's abrasive personality was sufficient to alienate a number of his colleagues. His feelings towards Sharon Stone are particularly complex. Stone claims that the pair have a distinct love-hate relationship. 'He loves me, and I hate him!' Verhoeven counters all her criticisms with some equally barbed remarks of his own. 'So goddamned mean – when she's angry she knows how to say things that really hurt.' His often peculiar working practices upset a number of people connected with the film. 'I have such a strong vision that when people deviate from it I get upset or irritated,' he admitted.

In the film community he is almost legendary for his need to get involved on the set. His urge to demonstrate the peculiar needs of the love scenes caused more than one altercation on the set, but Verhoeven is unrepentant. 'I felt it was so god-damned difficult to do, psychologically. The tension is so – I mean, taking your clothes off even if you have a set restricted to seven or eight people is still unpleasant.'

One example of his apparent duplicity caused something of a rift between Verhoeven and Sharon Stone. Soon after the start of the film comes a critical scene where the cop, played by Michael Douglas, brings Catherine (Sharon Stone) into the station to face questioning on the murder of her boyfriend. In a provocative short white dress she tantalizes and taunts the policemen as they interrogate her.

It is a sexy, arousing scene made all the more so when one remembers that the scene has been set up directly following a scene where Douglas and his partner meet Catherine Tramell and take her into the station. It is made perfectly obvious that beneath the white dress she is wearing no underwear. In the interrogation room, with one tantalizing flash of tanned legs crossing, her pubic hair is exposed to the camera's unrelenting gaze.

181

Verhoeven persuaded her to do this for the sake of the film by assuring her that the shot would not be unpleasant or too revealing. Despite her doubts Stone did as requested but the shot in the film realized her worst fears. It was her original idea for Catherine to flash the police in that way but, 'I wanted it to be alluded to, but not to get a bird's eye view.'

Verhoeven is not popular with the likes of Joe Eszterhas or Irwin Winkler or Sharon Stone but, perhaps surprisingly, Michael Douglas is lavish in his praise. 'I'd make another movie with Paul in a second. I think he's very, very talented – God forbid you'd go through a process like that with someone who's not!'

For his part Verhoeven was equally impressed by Douglas. 'I think Michael is extremely generous as an actor. He stays on the set to lend support through every take when other actors would go back to their trailers.'

Talking about the type of personality Douglas brought to the film Verhoeven was equally effusive. 'Michael is not afraid to bring forward the evil or shadowy sides of his personality, which we all have – and pretend not to have. I think he's a torn personality . . . And that's very attractive!'

The role played by Michael Douglas, Detective Nick Curran, is visibly a torn personality bordering on the psychotic, a bad-mouthing ex-cokehead and a very dangerous man nicknamed 'shooter' by his colleagues. 'In his recent past his wife committed suicide, he accidentally killed four tourists, and now he's undergoing therapy at police headquarters,' recalled Michael Douglas. 'This is a guy struggling with whether he has any worth at all. Then he meets Catherine, his match, somebody who takes him over to that dark side he knows so well, and she's an addictive personality too. You watch the struggle between his responsibilities as a police officer and his basic instincts, which are towards sex and violence.'

And the part allowed Douglas to display the one acting characteristic which makes him unchallenged in his profession. He seems able to take almost any part, however unpleasant, and make the audience see something sympathetic in the character.

We may find Nick Curran, or Dan Gallagher, or Gordon Gekko or Nick Conklin anti-social and hateful but through some special ability of Michael Douglas none of these characters seem totally flawed. In all of these parts the audience in the main seems to recognize something of 'there but for the grace of God . . .'

Sharon Stone was equally intrigued by the peculiar motivations of her character. 'Catherine is so raw and willing to go anywhere to pull Nick into her web. She'll seduce him in her mind. She'll seduce him with her sexuality. And when she sees that something "gets" him it makes her all the more excited.'

Those basic instincts are given full vein in the film which is happy to examine some of the darker human traits. Violence is an ever-present undercurrent in *Basic Instinct* even in the sex scenes. Michael Douglas encountered more criticism because of one of the other scenes in the film which protesters claimed was little more than a gratuitous example of date rape. The encounter between Douglas and police psychologist Beth Gardner by actress Jeanne Tripplehorn as 'a rough sex scene between two consenting adults. That's what we always called it!'

'The aggressiveness of it had us both nervous,' remembered Douglas. 'I was initiating the action and she went along. She's a great reactor and it went really well!'

'It was like a rodeo!' admitted Tripplehorn. 'It worked because we had these physical signposts to hit, and we could just be spontaneous, move around and fill it with intensity and emotion.'

The scene is almost lurid in its intensity and provoked a wave of accusations of date rape, and yet what is presented is initially more disturbing because it was so unexpected. Beth Gardner is ravished and overpowered by Nick Curran, but she doesn't throw him out of her apartment until much later. Whatever is happening is clearly a two-way process and they have obviously enjoyed a very physical relationship before this savage encounter. Her subsequent anger is not caused by the virtual rape he inflicted on her, but by his reaction to it. Their relationship has obviously been intense and this incident is a continuance not an aberration.

'I want to be with him – on his terms,' stated Tripplehorn, while Douglas defined the situation as 'It's not a question of her resisting and then just going along. It turns her on – she's excited!'

The tempestuous encounter between Nick Curran and Beth Gardner reached heights of excitement which surprised even Tripplehorn. The scene as written required Douglas to bite the back of her neck several times while he ravished her over the back of a chair. After Verhoeven had run through a handful of takes Tripplehorn approached Douglas and told him, 'You know, you can really bite me!' only to be told by Douglas, 'I am biting you!'

'I couldn't feel it!' admitted Tripplehorn. 'That's how involved we were. The next day the make-up people had to cover up the bruises!'

That scene, among several others, was criticized for its failure to take account of the AIDS controversy. Curran fails to take any precautions which, in the climate where safe sex is a lifesaver, seemed very unwise. 'We went back and forth on it, but we decided it's part of my character's self-destructive behaviour,' admitted Douglas. 'We didn't feel it was appropriate to get into current event issues. You could accuse us of being irresponsible, but I see this film as the equivalent of a smutty detective novel. It's well-structured and well written but I didn't read anything more into it.'

Tripplehorn was a relative newcomer to the demands of major films and her baptism could hardly have been more shocking or testing. 'I was really scared but Michael makes you feel at ease,' she admitted. 'He's very gentle and very professional – he'd check in after each take "Are you okay"?'

This respect for the sensitivity shown by Douglas is shared by the female star of the film, Sharon Stone. 'When we had to do parts of the sex scene that were . . . I don't know, shy-making – he made a lot of jokes and was really warm.'

Stone was clearly intimidated by Douglas, at least at the start of filming. 'Michael has a very powerful sexuality and almost a dangerous edge to his sexuality. He's also a huge movie star.'

The film became such an immediate success in the States that Sharon Stone quickly became a hot property but Douglas had seen it happening long before the final cut was approved. 'This movie will make her a star,' stated Douglas. 'She's now A-list competition for any actress in the world.'

This smacks a little of being wise after the event for Douglas had to be persuaded by Verhoeven that Stone could do it. 'I'm out there, and I'm not risking myself with some amateur!' snarled Douglas.

Stone was not an amateur but she had, prior to *Basic Instinct*, failed to make a big impact in

Hollywood. From a modelling background she made her first film appearance in Woody Allen's *Stardust Memories*. Later appearances in *Irreconcilable Differences* and *King Solomon's Mines* were more notable than her work in such epics as *Bay City Blues* or *The Vegas Strip Wars* or even *Police Academy IV*. She developed an unfortunate reputation as the 'nearly girl' as she nearly got major parts in *Dick Tracy*, *Havana* and *Batman*. Her chequered career eventually led to Arnold Schwarzenegger and Paul Verhoeven and *Total Recall*. Their relationship during the filming was so stormy that many movie insiders were surprised that Verhoeven recommended her for *Basic Instinct*.

Some fifty actresses were interviewed for the part including notable names like Ellen Barkin and Geena Davis. A clutch of name actresses like Greta Scacchi, Lena Olin and Michelle Pfeiffer refused to even read for the part but screen tests were provided for Mariel Hemingway among others. Sharon Stone was not initially a popular choice with Carolco or even with Michael Douglas but the glacial power of her work won over all doubters.

Her calculated decision some time ago to pose nude for *Playboy* purely to advance her career caused many people to suspect her integrity or motivation. Some insiders from the *Total Recall* set held the mischievous belief that Stone was typecast as Catherine. Paul Verhoeven did not argue against such a suggestion. Indeed he seemed to encourage it, observing cheerfully, '*Ja*, Sharon is Catherine without killing. That's a quote, isn't it?'

Discussing the actresses who turned down the Sharon Stone role Douglas remarked, 'With *Basic Instinct* these actresses could not get past the fact of Catherine's bisexuality. So I just smiled – revenge is a great motivator for me – and said, "OK, if we pull this off you ladies will only have created more competition for yourselves!" '

Stone now describes the teaming of herself and Michael Douglas as 'The Ginger Rogers and Fred Astaire of the 90s!' whilst in response, in a rare flash of humour, Paul Verhoeven says, 'Yeah, horizontal!' Sharon Stone herself entertained no doubts about the role, despite the nudity and the very explicit sex scenes. 'From the second I read the script I did everything I could to get this role,' she admitted. 'It's so rare that a female character is more than an appendage to some guy. But I never thought of Catherine as bisexual, or even sexual. Sex is just the currency she uses to get what she wants.'

'Michael was terrific,' stated Stone firmly. 'Supportive, protective, and always making jokes. When we were nude, we were more well-mannered and respectful to each other than when we had our clothes on.'

And the pair were nude frequently, featuring in some of the sexiest scenes ever released in a major

Hollywood production. Douglas had been happy to appear in the film for many reasons, not the least of which was the reputed $14 million fee. However, there were equally compelling artistic reasons for his involvement. 'I thought it would be fun to play a character with an edge. Nick has a hot temper. He tends to jump emotionally when he shouldn't. I know this is a time when we like to see our heroes as heroes but I'm still intrigued by that grey area in people.'

He was also attracted to the part because of its sexy nature. 'I just wanted to do it for the sexuality, for the fact of just doing a sexy-type picture.' However, he had forced a clause into his contract stipulating that he would not be shown full frontal. 'I wanted to leave something to the imagination.'

Despite mischievous rumours that Douglas used a body double for some of the nude scenes there was no replacement involved. It was all Michael Douglas, warts and all.

Little is left to the imagination in the scenes between Douglas and Tripplehorn but they were tame compared to what took place between Douglas and Sharon Stone. The reputed tendency of director Paul Verhoeven to indulge the prurient fantasies of his audience met full realization in *Basic Instinct*. Douglas and Stone co-operated fully in achieving Verhoeven's aims, but it wasn't always a comfortable process. And there were lots of people in the audience, given the stark realism of the sex scenes, who wondered just how much was acting. Douglas said:

> Making love is the act of losing control, losing yourself. But acting making love is choreographed, like dance steps or a fight scene. When she scratches your back, you have to arch two beats, three, then roll over, boom . . . that's what acting's about – making it totally believable, and simultaneously being aware of the moves and the technical aspects. Quite honestly, after the first ten or fifteen minutes of awkwardness, it's just marathon running. You have to be in great shape, because it's five or six days of the most exhausting scenes you could possibly do. It's not a turn-on at all!'

Despite his protestations he was obviously aware of the possible impact of the sex scenes on the audience, and on those closest to him. 'For Diandra it's difficult. It's one thing to see you kissing another actress up on the screen, and another thing to have really strong physical sex scenes.'

Such worries affected him during filming but his mind was quickly occupied by more immediate concerns. The tumult caused by the many protesters against *Basic Instinct* ran on, threatening, or possibly guaranteeing, the eventual success of the film.

A splinter protest group took its name from the surname of the murderer in the film and threatened to widely publicize the ending of the film. This policy was implemented by a range of bizarre practices such as the writing of the identity of the murderer in blood on the pavements outside cinemas showing the film. Other patrons held aloft posters stating the name of the murderer. Still more wore T-shirts proclaiming, on the front, 'Catherine Did It!' and on the back, 'Icepick Wielding Bisexual Fag-Dyke – Do Not Agitate!'

Revealing the identity of the murderer in the film would ruin the movie for many people. Queer Nation, the protest group responsible for the plan, believe that such a devious publicity campaign would persuade many thousands of people not to visit the film. The financial consequences could be dire and it was a threat taken very seriously by Carolco.

Protest groups took a number of extraordinary steps. One group planned to release moths inside cinemas so that the wings fluttering in front of projection booths would send giant shadows on the screens. Other protesters intended to picket cinemas across America and handing out leaflets protesting about the film. A typical leaflet on the east coast read, 'We think the movie could do us harm, by reinforcing ignorance about homosexuality and by providing an excuse for assaults on an escalating number of lesbians and gay men.'

And the controversy threw up another threat which clearly worried Michael Douglas in its long-term implications for the film industry. 'The whole thing is getting so politically convoluted,' stated Douglas wearily. 'It's important to make films which make a statement, but you can't make films which consider every view, every opinion!'

His female lead in *Basic Instinct* shared his unease at the artistic intolerance threatened by the film's notoriety. 'I respect their right to freedom of speech,' said Sharon Stone, talking of the protest groups like Queer Nation and the Gay and Liberal Alliance against Defamation. 'But they should also respect my freedom of expression as an artist.'

Watching the protests which sprang up like forest fires as the film opened Michael Douglas commented, 'I don't feel there is a true justification in the film for their actions. I support Gay Rights, I support any minority's rights, but I think this is truly uncalled-for!'

One of the more popular signs held up by the protesters read, 'Michael Douglas, Fuck You, Racist, Sexist, Anti-Gay'. The lack of truth in any of these accusations clearly upset him, as did the fact that neither Joe Eszterhas, who wrote the script, or Paul Verhoeven, who made the film, attracted any condemnatory signs.

All the troubles which beset the film touched a sensitive area in Douglas and he wasn't slow to latch onto one of the most important aspects of the film. 'I think it's a movie we've gotta get out there. Everything's so repressive now – it's like the No generation. You can't do anything, you can't eat anything, you have to abstain.'

The continuing protests, particularly in the wake of the Joe Eszterhas débâcle, forced Douglas into a series of comments on the situation. 'I've always totally supported gay rights. But this whole thing of being politically correct is really a bore. In movies somebody's got to be the villain and it can't always be the Italians!'

In another of the torrent of promotional interviews for the film Douglas was even more explicit. 'Should WASPs be the only villains? I mean, no Italians, no blacks – if there are no minorities that can have socially deviant behaviours. I don't get it!'

Another quote on this vexed subject touches on one of the most contentious problems afflicting American film-makers. 'We have an acceptance of violence in the US to an extent that would never exist in Europe. The question is, "Why won't we allow sex to be sexy?" '

And there is a perceivable weariness in his remarks about the long-term implications of the arguments about the film. 'I'm someone who's had my share of pictures that have had an impact, but I also reserve and demand the right to make two hours of entertainment without having to be the moral, social custodian of our society.'

He seemed grateful for a chance to comment on the film as a piece of cinema rather than as a moral statement, and he had some interesting observations on his role in the film.

> It reminds me a little of *Fatal Attraction*, not
> necessarily because of the sexuality but because
> you're carrying the storyline. You're in every
> single scene of the picture and you have to carry
> the suspense of the storyline. The other
> characters, in this Sharon Stone, and in the case
> of *Fatal Attraction* Glenn Close, they have these
> more colourful roles, they get to play the
> psychotic or a murder suspect and it's more
> colourful, so it was hard for me, this role was
> more of a reactive-type role.

His thoughts about the motivation for Nick
Curran are also illuminating. 'What I tried to do
was based upon Nick, my character's background
to create this sense of a volcano, that he could go
off at any possible time, and his destructive sense
for danger, his destructive sense of sexual
encounters, and his substance abuse with alcohol
and drugs.'

The characterizations of Curran, Tramel and
Gardiner intertwined in a provocative and
controversial film but once again the efforts of
protest groups to stop the public seeing a film had
the opposite effect. People were intrigued by the
controversy and came out in droves, in America
and Europe and elsewhere, to see the film which
was stirring up such a furore and visible
antagonism.

Paul Brett, Director of Marketing at Guild Film

Distribution in London, commented on the American problems. 'I think the protests in the States were very well structured but they've also backfired because they've ended up drawing more people to the film than otherwise might have seen it.' He also held firm views on the moral implications of the protests.

'And their argument is untenable – that gays should only be seen in "normal" roles and never portrayed as villains. The political correctness movement is really frightening because it's censorship of the worst kind and I categorically cannot see that this movie is going to encourage gay bashing!'

On its opening weekend *Basic Instinct* took a very healthy $15 million and the continuing furore threatened to make attendances rise dramatically. Within a week of release it became the number one box office draw in the United States.

The similarity between the titles *Fatal Attraction* and *Basic Instinct* is not entirely coincidental, and early indications suggest that Michael Douglas will again achieve mass popularity through a highly charged, sensual performance. At the time of the release of *Basic Instinct* he again found himself standing at a professional crossroads, able to choose roles at a time to suit his personal and business lives but still, like many of his peers, searching for another blockbuster role.

After *Basic Instinct* he was scheduled to go into

a new Joel Schumacher project, *Falling Down*, but that film was hit by the downturn in Hollywood's fortunes before filming even started. The reported $14 million fee received by Douglas for *Basic Instinct* was chopped to less than half for *Falling Down*. This was no reflection on his work on *Basic Instinct* or on the financial success of that film, but was rather a comment on the profligacy of Carolco.

Once again he opted for the meaty part, the bad guy, in the film despite being initially offered the main lead which went instead to Robert Duvall.

Basic Instinct is a massive, even notorious, success but even if *Falling Down* does not provide another mega-hit it may come in a long-cherished production which has been in Michael Douglas' mind for several years. A film starring both Michael and Kirk Douglas, father and son, and two of the biggest names in the film industry.

The idea for a joint film starring Michael and Kirk is not a new one. It was first mooted many years ago at the beginning of Michael's career. At that time he was understandably reluctant to get involved. 'The more I think of it the more I feel it would be a difficult idea to work out,' he admitted. 'They'd tend to interpret it as cashing in on my dad's name.'

As the years have progressed the likelihood of Michael ever being accused of cashing in on Kirk's name has receded if not entirely vanished.

The project now would be a promotional

dream, and one can imagine the mileage to be derived from interviews with both Kirk and Michael. Chat shows the world over would drool at the prospect of getting the pillars of the Douglas dynasty together to discuss their joint film and their turbulent lives. Major studios are already nibbling at the bait and the Douglas duo will ensure that the successful studio will pay heavily for the privilege of marketing the Michael-Kirk film.

Storylines are being considered and some work has already been done on scripting but the film is still in its embryonic stage. Both father and son are searching for a storyline which will 'reflect my dad's rags-to-riches story and my coming of age in the 60s'.

There is an element of urgency involved and that is caused by the one thing which all the Hollywood millions cannot overcome – age. Kirk is now in his mid-seventies. An active, hugely intelligent, still dynamic man but facing the inevitability of decline.

If the film uniting father and son is to be made then it must happen soon otherwise, sadly, Kirk may not be able, or even be around, to make it. Kirk's recent helicopter accident provided a sobering warning to his sons that their father's legendary toughness may be a thing of the past. Kirk was a passenger in a helicopter, piloted by Noel Blanc, which collided with a stunt plane on take-off from Santa Paula. Two men in the plane were killed. Kirk was seriously injured but fortunately made a full recovery, but the incident brought home to his family the fact that Spartacus wasn't immortal after all.

If Kirk and Michael do make their film together this projected film could even be the Douglas' equivalent of the Fondas' *On Golden Pond* when the aged Henry Fonda dragged one last performance out of the depths of his experience starring alongside and against his famous daughter.

A film co-starring Michael and Kirk would have eerie echoes of the delicacy of *Golden Pond* especially if it managed to capture that film's element of failed relationships and eventual reconciliation. That is a road which Michael and Kirk have walked, often stormily, and even though mutual reconciliation and forgiveness was long ago achieved in real life Hollywood could not refuse the chance of seeing such schmaltz realized on celluloid.

And there is the other massive prize to be considered. Henry Fonda received an Oscar for *Golden Pond*. Possibly unjustifiably, because his work on earlier films like *Grapes of Wrath* and *Mr Deeds* was clearly of great substance. Yet even if the award was stimulated more by sentiment than by merit nobody would contest that it was well deserved.

Which member of the Academy could refuse the opportunity to bestow on Kirk Douglas the one supreme honour, the Oscar, which he has always been denied? The pressure to name him Best Actor would surely be irresistible, and that alone will provide a massive reason to make the joint film.

That film could prove to be the next major landmark in the career of Michael Douglas and, given the massive interest it is certain to generate, it may finally establish him at the level that his work, and his ability, deserves.

Because, even after several hugely successful films and an Oscar and a string of lesser awards there is still the sense of something yet to be realized in Michael Douglas. He has endured the 'angry young man' years and is now playing virile, exciting leading men. What could be left?

Sherry Lansing has described Michael Douglas as having 'talent and a mysterous charisma'. This is undeniably true but despite his many achievements the man is an enigma and has been all his life. So many of his comments and quotes refer to himself as a chameleon and this aspect of personal inter-changeability is something which has preoccupied him for many years.

I think I'm a chameleon. I think it's something I possibly inherited early on as a child going back and forth between two families. I know that whether it's right or wrong I have an ability to sort of fit into a lot of different situations, and make people feel relatively comfortable in a wide range without giving up all my moral values. I think that same chameleon-like quality can be translated into films.

His background has possibly caused more introspection and self-analysis than is normal but given the influence of Kirk Douglas that cannot be surprising.

For many years Michael Douglas lived in the immense shadow of his father, but for a considerable time he has escaped that shadow to become a major star in his own right. Perhaps in the next decade the enigma which is Michael Douglas will start casting his own long shadows.

9 A Douglas Dynasty

Psychologists would find rich pickings in Kirk and Michael Douglas and their family. The scale of the triumphs achieved by father and son, and to a lesser extent the other sons, would be sufficient to cause immense pride in any family. And yet for a man as compulsively ambitious, as totally career-orientated as Kirk Douglas the success of Michael must have caused a violent mix of emotions. On the one hand a natural, instinctive pride at his son's accomplishments: on the other, darker hand is a maelstrom of meaner emotions prompted by professional pride and rivalry. Kirk Douglas, the generally admitted 'most unpopular man in Hollywood' and dutiful father, clearly loves his eldest son and is immensely proud of his achievements. At the same time Kirk Douglas, top gunslinger in town, has traditionally been resentful of any challenge to his natural supremacy. Back in 1959 Kirk Douglas admitted, 'These kids keep shoving . . . and shoving . . . and pretty soon they push the old-timers right off.' This resentment of challenges is deeply felt even when, in commercial terms, it comes from his own son.

Complicating the relationship between Kirk and Michael there is also the incalculable effect of the *One Flew Over the Cuckoo's Nest* situation. The project was Kirk's baby, something that he held onto with fierce, almost fatherly, pride for several years. He nurtured and protected and developed the idea of taking Kesey's book to the screen and despite a glowing Broadway success was denied the chance to realize his dream.

That would have been galling in itself but to find the project coming to such glittering fruition under the control of his precocious eldest son must have been dreadfully hard to take. The pain of losing the role of McMurphy has already been mentioned but the importance and long-term significance of that incident cannot be mistaken. The whole relationship between Kirk and Michael turned on that moment, and from that time onwards it was impossible for Kirk to denigrate or dismiss Michael or despair of his efforts.

It was just as inconceivable, from the time of *Cuckoo's Nest*, for Michael to regard his father with the same distant awe as he had always done. In one cascade of millions of dollars the young stag had overthrown the mastery of the old stag and their lives could never be the same again.

The Oscar picked up by the exultant Jack Nicholson for *Cuckoo's Nest* rubbed further salt into the wound, and the scar tissue had hardly formed when the Academy delivered another mortal snub to Kirk by awarding Michael the Best Actor Oscar for *Wall Street*.

In both respects Michael, the actor/producer, achieved something which Kirk desperately desired and some feeling of resentment and anger would be almost inevitable. The fact that the dirty deeds were done by Michael, the elder son, was some compensation but psychologists recognize in this situation the classic stimulus for a trauma.

'Following Jung, many psychologists and people in those fields did work on parent-sibling rivalry, and the facts presented about the Kirk-Michael Douglas relationship certainly pose a number of fascinating questions!' commented a leading practitioner.

Many of Kirk's statements over the years indicate his concern about the emotional baggage his sons have had to carry around all their lives. It is no coincidence that most of these comments relate to Michael. Since the time of *Cuckoo's Nest*, as a famous actor and producer in his own right, Michael has attracted massive publicity and interest and it is inevitable that interviewers discussing fatherhood with Kirk would focus their questions on Michael.

Yet how often must Michael's brother and half-brothers have been disturbed and annoyed by the constant references to him, particularly when so much of their father's attention seemed glued to just one of the sons? Eric, Peter and Joel had just emerged from the tunnel of adolescence when it must have seemed that nobody was interested in them as individuals save as conduits to their famous father. Then they discovered the situation replaying with brother Michael, now the sole focus of attention.

This is a complex psychological situation for any family grouping but to it must be added the shameful dose of anti-semitism which blighted Kirk's formative years. In Amsterdam, where Kirk was raised, work opportunities were limited by economic conditions because of the depression. More particularly those opportunities were brutally restricted by racial limitations. 'At least there was no hypocrisy about it. I couldn't get a job delivering newspapers because I was a Jew, and no Jew was allowed to work at the largest factory in town.'

This disgraceful prejudice was even in evidence at college, supposedly the repository of more informed attitudes. During his four-year term at St Lawrence, Kirk was elected president of the student body. This was a real break with tradition for that establishment as Jews were effectively excluded from many college activities. Because of his sudden elevation in status one of the fraternity houses offered to allow him certain house privileges. 'I could pay dues, eat meals, live at the house, even attend fraternity dances. But I could not attend their meetings, and I guess they

204

wouldn't have taught me the secret handshake. I declined the kind invitation.'

Another major factor in the emotional picture must be Kirk's almost-savage adherence to the ancient Jewish zeal to become master of one's own fate. He still remembers an old saying of his mother's, 'As a Jew you will always have to be twice as good to get ahead in life.'

It is only the occasional ceremony which indicates the depth of his Jewish affinities. Thus in December 1989 Kirk and Michael were joint recipients of the Sheba Humanitarian Award from a group named The Friends of Tel Hashomer. There are similar social contacts between Michael and a number of other Jewish support groups although he carefully distances himself from any overt connection.

The final element in Kirk's complex psychological make-up is the almost mythical level of poverty suffered by his family until he eventually achieved some solid acting success. As his second wife, Anne, wryly commented, 'The only thing that would ever destroy my husband would be to find anybody as poor as he says he was. There are some but in his mind he was the poorest, most miserable child that ever lived.'

As the eldest son of this complex man Michael has carefully shielded the depth of his feelings and the extent of his commitment from public gaze. Since his early days in the industry when his tongue was unleashed too easily and too often, he has been much more guarded in his comments on matters outside filming.

Even Kirk recognizes the protective walls which Michael has erected over the years. 'There are layers that Michael has that I have never – I'm his father – been able to penetrate.' A series of carefully considered, delicately-weighted remarks have appeared from Michael on topics ranging from politics to the environment but he rarely lets the shield masking his true self slip.

Not surprisingly it is outsiders who have the intimate knowledge, and the distance, to pin the man down. Jimmy Webb, songwriter of hits like 'Up, Up and Away' and 'MacArthur Park', has been a close friend for many years. 'Sometimes I think he's very happy with himself,' he surmised. 'Sometimes I think he's very lonely.'

Other people who have worked with him are also bemused by the Douglas relationship. 'Michael's rather elusive,' stated Glenn Close. 'I'm very fond of him – he's a complicated man, very smart. There is a huge protected place in him – but look where he comes from.'

There are compelling reasons for seeing Michael Douglas as a younger version of his father. The same stubbornness, the same fierce independence, the same entrepreneurial flair, and yet he is clearly his own man. The path he has chosen to tread has been his own, and there are few people who now would dispute the wisdom of his various career choices.

The drive which has taken Kirk and Michael to the summit of their profession is clearly in the genes. There are a number of comments, particularly from Michael, which indicate the depth of feeling which connects, and perhaps at one time divided, them. 'My dad's got a Beverly Hills mansion with a big fence around it – and around himself too. He drove so hard to get where he's at that it turned people off. He never learned to take it easy . . . I never want to become that way.'

All his life Michael has been intent on taking time to enjoy life. Kirk didn't; his son won't make the same mistake.

He has been astute enough to study his father's career and learn valuable lessons. 'They used to make many more films back then, and sometimes you didn't get a chance to stop. He'd finish one picture and have to start another. He never got to enjoy his success. My big thing in life is, whatever you do, you have to stop when things are good and taste it.'

On another occasion he explored the same territory, in terms which suggested the exorcism of painful and long-standing ghosts. In later years he was proud of the fact that he had never resorted to therapy but at times it seemed that he was undergoing painful self-analysis by means of interview. 'I'm not being critical, I merely wanted to make clear the difference . . . I don't come off with the toughness of my father, but I do have the same amount of drive.'

He has long since realized the weight of responsibility that Kirk inadvertently hung round his eldest son's neck. 'I think I needed that distance from my father in age and time to really grow into myself!'

He has been dogged, particularly in his early years in the business, by the comparisons between Kirk and himself. 'My father carved out a very strong image early in his career, and it took me a while to carve out a niche for myself. I've talked to people like Charlie Sheen about the same problem.'

As Michael has reached his middle years he suffers an increasing number of comparisons with, and references to, his father. This cannot be surprising. Of all Kirk's sons Michael is the only one who truly resembles him, and there are an increasing number of moments in films when something in the cast of the eye or the turn of the jawline makes Michael look staggeringly like his father. The voice, softer and more modulated than Kirk's, still carries echoes of the Douglas twang. In looks and voice and even occasional mannerisms Michael can occasionally provide a chilling reminder of the great screen days of his father.

Most people's memory and image of Kirk Douglas is captured timelessly on celluloid. In the early sixties the granite-boned action man of *Spartacus* and *The Vikings* was approximately the same age as Michael now.

Comparisons between father and son are inevitable. Media hacks and industry moguls are particularly prone to linking the two. The ubiquitous Mike Medavoy stated, 'They're both very sexual men – just go back and look at Kirk's early work and look at Michael's. Peas in a pod.'

The publication of *The Ragman's Son*, Kirk's seminal autobiography, had a major impact on Michael. 'It gave me a clearer picture of where his rage came from. I have a clearer picture of what anti-Semitism meant to him. Also that he never got the approval he wanted from his father. I knew all that, but never as clearly as when I read the book.'

In a poignant way the book must have helped Michael reach a deeper understanding of some of his own problems. He remains aware, painfully aware of difficulties in his youth. 'I shuffled through life day to day as a pretty shy kid, pretty withdrawn, not a lot of confidence, a lot of fantasy, big dreams, very little reality.' Lack of confidence is a theme to which he consistently alludes, and it is obvious that he feels that he has suffered because of his chronic lack of self esteem. He was well into his twenties before he was able to feel good about himself, and Kirk's vast wealth and prestige couldn't help his son in that vital respect.

His father has had many occasions to ponder on the workings of his mysterious, powerful son, especially over the years that Michael was achieving a position of influence in the industry. 'Michael is enigmatic. He was enigmatic as a child, he's still enigmatic. Do you know Michael has never once asked me for money. Never once. Now that's insulting. I'm his father!'

On another occasion Kirk expanded on this theme. 'I think Michael's held in a lot of things. You see, I always felt Michael to be very enigmatic. It's only within the past eight years or so that I feel we're beginning to get closer. I always felt there were slight reservations in our relationship, you know? And I don't remember him confiding in me very much, which hurt me in a way.'

The pain Kirk suffered at losing his sons as a result of the divorce has rarely been examined, but it is there, it is real, and it has been an important element in moulding the character of Michael Douglas.

Kirk obviously had thought very hard about the various responsibilities of being a father. He has spoken movingly of his thoughts on this subject.

I worry whether my career places too much of a burden on my children. A parent's responsibility is to help a child function and find expression as a person. Functioning and finding expression sometimes comes hard to the children of so-called celebrities. They find themselves with a built-in handicap when they try to attain their own identity.

Asserting a personality is incredibly difficult when it is done in the shadow of great wealth and world fame. It is to Kirk's credit that he so clearly recognizes the difficulties; it is a tribute to Michael that he has overcome them. Yet both father and son are in a most unusual position because of their privileged lives. Normal patterns of social behaviour are unknown thanks to the wealth and fame from which neither has ever been able to escape.

Demonstrating his concern for his sons Kirk Douglas even went to the surprising lengths of discussing the problems of raising such a family with Joseph Kennedy, patriarch of the Kennedy clan. The aged ex-ambassador advised him to 'make your boys independent and then they will come back to you'.

Kirk took Kennedy's advice and acted on it. Some might say too enthusiastically. He brought his family up as a close-knit unit and their interdependence has grown over the years. Talking about Michael in 1973 Kirk stated that his son was 'a very talented actor and he'll function. In my family that's the key word. All I ever said to my sons is function!' The natural air of competition between four sons and stepsons has slightly diminished as maturity has set in, but Kirk instilled in all of them the desire to win, to be first.

In that respect the comparison between the Douglas dynasty and the Kennedy family is very well-drawn. A clutch of sons pushed towards success and excellence, with various strings occasionally pulled to smooth their various paths. One of the wry remarks made by Kirk after the Oscar ceremony came when, putting his arm round his son, he remarked, 'If I'd known he was going to be so successful I'd have been nicer to him as a kid.'

The names of Kirk and Michael Douglas are now so commensurate with fabulous wealth that it is difficult to appreciate that both were born into less than wealthy circumstances. At the time of Michael's birth in September 1944 his parents had been married exactly ten months. The wedding, on 2 November 1943, was but one of thousands of wartime weddings prompted by the onset of hostilities and, among the forces, the sudden realization of mortality.

The marriage between Kirk Douglas and Diana Dill was slightly different from many other wartime marriages in that the couple had known each other prior to the war. They had been students together at the American Academy of Dramatic Art where they had dated casually.

Diana Dill was the daughter of the Attorney General of Bermuda, part of one of the island's most established and prominent families. She had received an expensive education in a number of prestigious English establishments. Such an elegant childhood provided a stark contrast with Kirk's upbringing. He was the son of an immigrant peddler in Amsterdam, New York state, and the only son in a desperately poor family of seven children.

'My parents were Russian immigrants who couldn't read or write when they came to America. It was I who taught my mother to write her name,' remembered Kirk. 'My father peddled fruit in New York, and in his spare time had us children. Seven in all. Six girls and me. It was one helluva struggle, and there were times when we weren't sure where the next meal was coming from.'

It was from two such unlikely sources that the marriage was spawned, and the resulting children, Michael and Joel, were the product of the union of two highly different worlds. Many of the problems which afflicted the marriage were the result of Kirk's fanatical desire to escape poverty forever. Strains between the couple began to develop and Kirk's strange personality quirks would eventually divide them. However, it was during one period of marital normality that Kirk received the news that he was a father for the first time. His first child, a son, had been born at 10.30 a.m. on the morning of 25 September 1944.

Although Diana wished to call the baby Kirk Douglas Junior the father was totally set against the idea. 'I have never liked the idea of junior,' he observed. The name Michael became the parental choice but as a measure of compromise they placed the initial 'K' as part of the baby's name.

213

Kirk's refusal to entertain the possibility of naming his son Kirk Douglas Junior may not be unconnected with the fact that in the orthodox Jewish religion a child is never named after a living family member.

Despite the happiness brought by the children the tensions within the marriage were building frantically, and the difference in attitudes and temperaments were becoming obvious. Very enigmatically Kirk Douglas once told Diana, 'You're always happy unless something comes along to make you unhappy. I'm always unhappy unless something comes along to make me happy. And then I'm not sure that I'm happy.'

The gulf between Kirk and Diana had been growing remorselessly wider, and eventually reached a point where separation was inevitable. They had become strangers, and the divisions between them had been growing virtually since the wedding. Kirk's public remarks were not calculated to endear him to an intelligent, perceptive woman like Diana. 'Women should train themselves to complement men. I'm appalled by how little women know about how to run a home . . . I may be too proud of men but I'm convinced they're superior to women.'

The question of her working had been a source of major disagreement between them during the marriage but had grown ever more bitter as they grew older. As Diana remarked, 'My wanting to act was an assertion of my own independence –

maybe in defiance of Kirk's success, maybe in defence of it.'

The divorce of Kirk and Diana came in February 1950 when Michael was just five years old. His life then became a shuttle between two sides of a continent and two hugely different lifestyles. Kirk remained in Beverly Hills in splendid isolation; Diana moved back to New York with Michael and Joel.

It was a moment of supreme sadness for Kirk. 'It never occurred to any of us then that my sons might live with me, or even that they might want to live with me. I would fly back every chance I got, and they would spend summer vacations, and often Christmas and Easter, with me.'

The forced move to New York allowed Diana to assert her independence as a newly divorced single parent. It also allowed her to chisel out an identity for herself, one which had been denied her during the latter years of the marriage. To Kirk Douglas everybody lived in his shadow and he simply couldn't comprehend his wife wanting to come out of that shadow to find a patch of sunlight for herself.

Diana rationalized the move to the east coast in terms of career opportunities. 'I went to New York to do a television drama and decided I wanted to live in the East where I could start again. Luckily I found an apartment near Central Park. I furnished it myself and converted the dining room into a playroom for the boys.'

The apartment on Central Park West became home during the boys' childhood. Michael went to the Alan Stevenson school on 78th Street, an academic establishment which insisted on a definite school uniform with white shirt, blazer, tie and grey flannels. The strictness of the uniform and behaviour regulations was a help in those difficult early days in New York. It provided Michael with an anchor, and it also reflected the concerns of his mother with correct standards, but contrasted starkly with casual attitudes in California.

His mother's insistence on a full but disciplined education would take Michael to old-established pre-prep schools like Deerfield Academy in Massachusetts and Choate, an Ivy League prep in Wallingford, Connecticut.

Perhaps curiously Diana was always an actress. When Michael was six and Joel was just four she went to India for almost two months to film *Monsoon*, leaving them in Manhattan with the housekeeper. The boys were happily raised in a household where summer stock and films and Broadway were constant elements and regular topics of conversation. The business enabled mother and famous son to achieve one notable pairing for long after Michael had grown into a man Diana was to play a minor role in one of his early films, *The Star Chamber*.

Naturally Diana watched the boys closely to see how the divorce affected them. 'When we were first divorced Michael had a lot of anger. He still has a lot of residual anger. It's a warring thing in him, but he's a very kind person and it disturbs him.'

Years after the divorce from Kirk she met another man while involved in summer stock at Chagrin Falls, Ohio. Her subsequent remarriage to William Darrid, theatrical producer and writer, came in December 1956 and brought some much-needed stability to the family. 'Bill was a moral rock for Michael and his brother, Joel. They always knew what they could count on. We treated them with respect and expected respect in return.'

Diana was most impressed by the enthusiasm with which Bill took on Michael and Joel. 'If you don't want kids yourself it's hard to take responsibility for someone else's,' she has since admitted.

The influence of Kirk Douglas stretched a considerable way and the children of his first marriage were to find that, thanks to Kirk's growing reputation, his shadow even extended across America. Many painful years would pass before Michael was able to assert his complete independence, but with the move to the east coast the pattern of Michael's life was set. 'We had to develop an emotional toughness travelling between our two different worlds!' he recalled.

He was the son of an increasingly famous father, but they were separated by a continent both geographically and emotionally. And they were also distanced by the perception of Kirk as a man of heroic stature, a twenty-foot giant freeing slaves and warring against evil. In real life he was often cruel, selfish and over-demanding, prone to such ridiculous flashes of macho behaviour as getting his sons to punch him in the belly to prove how strong he was.

For any sensitive child to grow through childhood, adolescence and puberty in the shadow of such a towering figure must have been very hard. Almost inevitably Michael started to withdraw, to hide part of himself away. 'I was not very happy. I was an introverted, uptight kind of kid,' stated Douglas in a telling admission.

'I just didn't let anyone rattle my cage. I was trying to live my own life,' recalled Douglas. 'I didn't give out too easily!' That habit of secrecy became so engrained that he has never entirely been able to lose it. As an actor it is very useful but in his personal life he has had to suffer the suspicion from many people that he is not able, or willing, to give himself completely. To understand the reasons therapists or psychologists would look back almost forty years to the time when a 5-year-old boy watched his parents separate and divorce and spent night after night crying for his parents to get back together again.

In a historical echo of earlier problems between Kirk and his father, Herschel, Michael was distanced from his father by a sense of alienation which would not fade for decades.

He doesn't try to evade responsibility for his part in the problems. 'Back then reality was a stranger to me. I was all show and superficial as hell,' admitted Michael. 'My life had been about getting through, not making waves, being a chameleon. When I was with my mother I lived a New England prep school existence. Summers with my father in Hollywood, life was so different. Just tell me how you wanted me to be and I was it!'

This obvious insecurity dogs his thoughts and words, and has done for almost a quarter of a century. 'Coping stops you from much self analysis or explanation. I hide behind my work a lot. When I talk about being a chameleon it means basically reflecting who you are with at the time. You are always protecting yourself!'

Any analysis of the difficulties besetting the Kirk-Michael relationship must admit that they are the legacy of the fraught situation between Kirk and his father, Herschel, half a century earlier. Kirk's second wife, Anne, perceptively remarked, 'Part of my husband's life has been a monstrous effort to prove himself and gain recognition in the eyes of his father.' It would not be inaccurate or a wild exaggeration if Michael's wife, Diandra, were to make the same remark. Kirk's first wife, Diana, has described the Kirk-Michael relationship as 'a question of the old stag versus the young stag'. Their battle is as old

219

as life itself but time decrees that there will only be one victor.

Much of Michael's behaviour as a young man was not calculated to inflame his father, but it still had that effect. Michael turned down Yale and his initial decision to choose college in California rather than anywhere else in America sent Kirk apoplectic, if only for the reasons which his son cheerfully gave. 'I saw a brochure for the University of California which had a surfer and two bikini-wearing girls on the cover. In 1963 bikinis were almost unknown especially in New York. I also heard the rumour that UC had a ratio of three girls to every boy. So I went there.'

Michael Douglas wasn't the only boy in history to go slightly wild when confronted with the licence of college after the fetters of school. After two terms the University of California asked him to vacate the premises after a series of unimpressive results. Eventually he would return to such glowing effect that he would be made Alumnus of the Year, but the time when the college invited him to depart was the first of a succession of low points. By any standards it was a failure, and Kirk didn't appreciate failure especially when it was visited on his doorstep in California.

In an attempt to cool the developing rancour Michael headed back east and took a job at a Mobil gas station. This unlikely vocation was greatly aided by a deep-rooted love of automobiles which he supplemented by joining a hot rod club, the Downshifters. During the period working for Mobil he received the famous plaque for Employee of the Month, and this first award travelled back west with him as he headed up into the mountains to the commune and his first adult home.

He was a boy who needed love but didn't, couldn't get it from Kirk so he gratefully took that affection from his surrogate family in the commune. In many ways Michael now sees the whole period in the Hollywood Hills bathed in a warm glow of nostalgia. The commune became his extended family compensating for the myriad insecurities caused by his natural family. And most of those insecurities were prompted, however unwittingly, by his famous father despite the devotion to his sons which must never be underestimated. He loved his children but his adherence to a fierce ethic meant that he would not allow himself to show it. Spartacus was many things but he was not a New Man.

'He has a sense of loyalty and responsibility to his family which borders on a guilt complex,' commented a family friend. 'You don't have to be a psychiatrist to realize that this is a compensation for his own father's lack of loyalty and responsibility. Kirk is first and foremost a family man.'

As he grew to maturity Michael was able to develop a deeper understanding of what afflicted Kirk when his sons were young. 'Kirk felt a tremendous responsibility in being a father and very guilty because he was divorced,' admitted Michael.

> Because Kirk's father abandoned his family when he was young he felt really bad. So when we visited each other over the holidays, he'd have this intense desire to be a father, do all the father things. It was difficult. It put a lot of pressure on him and a lot of pressure on us, because it wasn't like sharing time, it was playing a role.

Having his own child has also enabled Michael to appreciate the importance of the contacts he and Kirk did have. 'When my mother and father got divorced they each remarried . . . and the four of them are best friends. I guess it depends on what you're used to. I'm not saying that it's easy but if you've treasured the time you've spent with someone you'll want to stay in touch.'

Since Michael achieved his own fame Kirk has often been required to comment on his famous son's early life, and his words invariably have a tinge of sadness. 'When Diana and I divorced Michael was old enough to be affected. Only in the last few years have we become friends and I feel a warmth!'

During those 'last few years' perhaps Kirk has stopped judging his failures too harshly, and maybe Michael has begun to appreciate just how hard a task Kirk faced. Michael has loudly protested about being separated from Cameron because of filming; Kirk was separated from his sons for long stretches every year and had little choice in the matter.

And Michael Douglas has grown into fatherhood determined that his son is spared the anxieties suffered by Kirk's sons. 'Number one, my wife and I are together, which is a rarity in his age group. More than half his classmates' parents are divorced. I don't make as many movies as Kirk did, so there's more time. I think I'm just completing my twenty-first film – I'm never going to get close to his seventy!'

There was pride, but also a measure of sadness, in his words, 'At least Cameron's not bouncing and juggling between two families!'

Kirk Douglas has often been broodily reflective on earlier problems. 'I think very often I was harder on Michael and Joel because I was spending split time with them. One of the ways a father can show he cares is by bawling the hell out of them,' he admitted. 'I thought, well maybe one day they'll remember I wasn't indifferent to them. I wasn't there with a whip, but I think I have a much warmer relationship with my kids now than I did then.'

The influence of Kirk on that family has not always been positive. From the early years of growing up with a film star hero as a father, through the divorce, and beyond the stepfather years, both Michael and Joel suffered immense traumas as a direct result of family troubles particularly the direct influence of their father, the film superstar.

Both of them confess to the schizophrenic effect of visiting the movie set and seeing their father do apparently extraordinary things then go home and do ordinary things. Both brothers found such wide divergences in behaviour hard to deal with. Joel still talks amusingly about both brothers running screaming from the screening of *Lust for Life* when Vincent van Gogh, their dad, cut off his ear.

On another occasion Michael wandered on to the set of *The Bad and the Beautiful* when he was about eight years old. His father was shooting a hot love scene with Lana Turner. 'I was just watching and watching, and my dad looked up past the camera – and caught my eye. The wall totally broke. He quickly suggested I go outside.'

In a stark example of *déjà vu* Michael has been forced to have a long chat with his own son, Cameron, about *Basic Instinct*, conscious of the impact such graphic scenes could have on a young mind. 'It's an infidelity, I think, to his mother. The idea of Mum and Dad kissing or being involved with someone else is a bit shocking, so I think it's in defence of his mother. When I saw my dad in *The Bad and the Beautiful* I was shocked because there's a reality about love scenes in the movies that's different from shooting somebody which you know is only make-believe.'

The constant sense of schizophrenia was compounded by the fact that both brothers spent school times on the east coast with their mother and holiday times in California with Kirk. This pattern caused great disruptions in the boys' lives. In a telling admission Michael's brother, Joel, admitted, 'I would cry on the plane going west and I would cry on the plane going east.'

When they returned from periods with their father the boys would be generally unruly, throwing their clothes around and asserting that their father had a butler to deal with such things. 'I had to keep a strong grip on them,' remembered Diana, who is careful not to let slip the hurt which such incidents must have caused.

The boys established a strong bond between them. The frequency with which the pair have worked together is evidence of the depth of their enduring relationship. At one of the lowest professional points of his life, in the chaos of Morocco in 1975, the first person Michael turned to in his despair was brother Joel. Other relationships have proved less solid. He is a popular, affable man but he is very careful about letting people get too close. 'My stepfather told me when I was young – junior high school, and so worried about being popular – if you can count your friends on one hand you're lucky. I found that incredible at the time.'

Any major film star is surrounded by sycophants and deep adulation. Many have had their heads turned by such open adoration but Douglas has been more circumspect than most stars of his status. 'I think particularly because of the kind of business we're in, all this idolatry and public exposure, we tend to be cautious about making new friends. I tend to count and rely on the old ones.'

He would now class among his oldest friends his wife, Diandra, but the much-reported problems between Michael and Diandra have provided fodder for the gossip writers for almost twenty years. Their ten-month split after the *Romancing the Stone* and *Jewel of the Nile* filming demonstrated the extent of their marital difficulties. Yet the way they communicated throughout that testing period proved that there was an underlying caring which would survive the temporary difficulties.

As she commented plaintively at the time, 'Michael is away for such long stretches of time. Cameron is my best friend.'

For his own part, at another time, Michael commented, 'My work is a labour of love. Maybe that's why each project takes so long to do. I stick with it from beginning to end.'

On another occasion he commented, 'There was a time when nothing but show business interested me, but since my marriage that's no longer true. I used to think marriage would be a chore. It isn't. My marriage makes me happy – and that's from a guy who used to run from commitment!'

This statement seems a strong and touching

declaration but must be a public relations exercise. Less than two months after the interview containing these words was published Michael and Diandra entered on yet another lengthy separation. The fact that they got back together again was most important but the situation threw into doubt the seriousness of his printed words and intentions.

It has never been an easy marriage, particularly for Diandra. 'I wasn't the most understanding husband,' admitted Michael. 'And I have to agree that I haven't spent enough time at home.' After their wedding she was plunged into a hectic lifestyle for which she had had no training and very little knowledge. She has also had to live with a succession of lurid stories from women claiming to have had torrid affairs with her husband. 'There were women telling Diandra they were having an affair with me!' stormed Douglas. 'Women I'd never even met!'

'I was shocked at first,' she stated. 'But to me women claiming to be intimate with Michael are no different from women who run up to you in restaurants and shout "Darling!" when you haven't the vaguest idea who they are. You just take it with a pinch of salt.'

Michael Douglas has made it clear that he is disturbed by such incidents, especially by their profusion and regularity. 'There have been times when I've had to deal with innuendo or rumour that I was involved with somebody who I may never have even known. It's hard too on my family. A couple of times I've tracked somebody down and followed up on it.'

Given this enjoyment in extracting revenge one wonders just what steps the powerful Mr Douglas has taken in the course of 'following up on it'.

Both Michael and Diandra have been disturbed and hurt by frequent suggestions in the media that Michael has inherited his father's legendary capacity for women. Stories linking Michael Douglas with any one of a rack of beautiful women have been rife for almost twenty years. There have been so many stories that the reader is led to one of two inevitable conclusions. Either all, or at least some of the stories are accurate, or the press realize what an attractive and interesting target is Michael Douglas.

Some of the more durable rumours of an affair inevitably concerned Kathleen Turner. The long weeks away in Mexico filming *Romancing the Stone* started the rumours, which were later fuelled, without any substance, by the couple's subsequent work on *Jewel of the Nile* and *War of the Roses*.

Such eminently reliable publications as the *National Enquirer* went into great front-page detail about the Douglas marriage. That story cited an alleged relationship with Sabrina Guinness, a member of the British aristocracy, who could list past encounters with characters as unlikely as Jack Nicholson, Mick Jagger and Prince Charles.

The *Enquirer* story delivered a damning verdict

on Diandra. Quoting an unnamed 'inside source' the story claimed that she had refused divorce because 'she enjoys being Mrs Michael Douglas. Married to a hot actor she knows that most of her entrée to the most exclusive parties and social events is because of the glitter and power of her husband.'

Other comments in such publications as *People* magazine were equally offensive. 'They look like an S&M couple. She's wearing the dog collar. He married her for her looks and never lets her forget it.'

Perhaps such offensive nonsense is part of the price that people like Douglas must pay for their wealth and fame, but it must occasionally be difficult to bear.

The couple moved to California from New York and back again to try to improve their lives, to escape the incessant pressures. The shift in 1984 brought a degree of settlement and contentment to their lives. Michael was then able to devote himself to work which became increasingly New York orientated.

He was also able to wallow in the realization that his wife was developing a life in New York. 'Diandra blossomed into this extraordinary lady. She worked for charity and the Metropolitan Museum of Art and she modelled.'

Diandra found herself free to immerse herself in a number of good works including a commitment to fund-raising on behalf of the

Metropolitan Museum. She also worked with the Red Cross on a glittering première of *Jewel of the Nile*. A dinner and raffle provided almost a quarter of a million dollars for the charity. Such work gave her quite a profile and in New York she became a separate force in her own right. Talking of her husband and her many social functions she admitted, 'a lot of the time he simply doesn't want to go. If he is not inclined I don't see why he should. But then I will go. And usually I go alone. I've always been very independent.'

She has since extended those activities and on occasions can be found modelling, particularly at the charity functions in New York, Aspen and Los Angeles. At other times she assists various committees working with the homeless showing particular concern for the plight of the dispossessed in New York City. She has also developed an expertise in the production of documentary film which provides an interesting link between the activities of husband and wife.

Their difficulties hadn't vanished but success and maturity, and an undeniable devotion to their son, meant that there were fewer occasions when separation seemed to be necessary. Yet Diandra would still speak wistfully about the situation.

The bottom line is that we like each other. I try to be supportive of his work, which is an enormous burden he carries. And he is supportive of me.

And it's interesting, now he has to deal with my career pursuits.

Perhaps it's just a defence mechanism I have developed for peace of mind, but I don't feel jealousy anymore. I guess my theory is this: If Michael decides he loves another woman, I'd accept that. I wouldn't want to be with someone who didn't want to be with me.

This bleak statement sounded ominous, and the harbingers of doom launched into further gloomy pronouncements on the marriage. A perceptive analysis of the couple and their marriage will reveal that there is a third force, a mistress, lurking in the background. And yet it is not a human agent who presents a threat to Michael and Diandra. It is his work, his almost obsessive commitment to the work.

Yet she has come to terms with the fact that his work is essential to him, and not a threat to her. 'I can look after myself now. I'm a very strong character. Michael's always had to go away on different projects. There was a time I didn't like that. Now I can cope. It all boils down to this; the best marriages are between people who can function on their own.'

Describing their initial problems he is brutally honest about the major difficulty. 'It's been very hard. I married Diandra when she was only nineteen years old. She not only was going through a growing-up process of her own but was married to this guy who was like blitzkrieg – totally absorbed and obsessed by making movies.'

Many years later the problems were not markedly different. 'Finding a good script is like falling in love with a girl,' he commented wryly. 'You read a script like you see a girl. You flirt with her a little bit and then you're hooked. You can't get her out of your mind, and that's what happens with my projects. It takes so long to make sure it's the right one.'

The only difference is that maturity and success, the undoubted lure of his family, has brought him to examine his priorities. He now manages a sensible compromise between work and home, throwing himself wholeheartedly into a project when it arises but ruthlessly closing the door on the business and its many tentacles between projects.

He has worked hard at balancing his commitments in his private and public lives. 'When I'm working that's my priority, and when it's over we spend time together. Of course they come and visit me on the set. The big dilemma is that I love my work – it's very rewarding to me – so it's just a matter of finding time for a break.'

He is a man who has searched his soul for justifications for his chosen career. Comments on the reasons for doing *Basic Instinct* betray a great deal about his philosophy. 'I'm attracted to the struggle in all of us between good and evil, and I see a dark side, a primitive side, a basic instinct side that we all have in ourselves and a cultured and sophisticated and humanitarian side, and I find life generally is a struggle between these two elements.'

And yet they are not completely on their own. Cameron, their only child, has become a most powerful unifying force. Michael had adopted the fashionable role of house-husband after the completion of work on *China Syndrome*. Diandra was able to continue college while Michael stayed home with Cameron. Bringing up baby was a long-established Hollywood classic, and Michael slipped happily into the role. 'I stayed with Cameron and was able to create a bonding which carried me through the periods when I've had to be apart from him.'

That bonding has continued and father and son are very frequently seen together. Friends of the family suspect that Michael is intent on developing so strong a relationship with his son that the problems which distanced him from Kirk will not and cannot recur. Cameron has even been enrolled in Eaglebrook, Michael's old prep school in Massachusetts, 'so he'll learn discipline'. However, as Cameron has already declared an interest in acting and a desire to follow in his father's, and grandfather's wake, Douglas has ruefully admitted, 'I suppose I should be flattered.'

And so Michael and Diandra are still together, celebrating their fifteenth wedding anniversary on the day *Basic Instinct* opened in America. Perhaps they can still find the detachment to smile at all the stories and rumours and confident predictions of divorce. One of the basic truths of the newspaper business is that 'good news is no news' and there is the suspicion that the Douglas marriage, if happy, would not provide copy for the papers and magazines. Normal people, devoid of the jaundiced savagery of the gossip columnists, would probably believe that in his personal life as in his professional career Michael Douglas has just about got it right.

Comments about his wife are frequent and flattering and quite touching. 'We struggled through all the things that happened with a fourteen-year age gap – what with me being in show business and her just being nineteen and finding out about life. Then we kind of grew together. I continue to have a deeper and deeper appreciation of Diandra and thank her for her strengths. I'll be eternally grateful to her – she's given me a security I might otherwise have thrown away!'

Despite his massive material successes Michael Douglas is demonstrably grateful for the qualities which Diandra has brought to his life. 'She's very intelligent. She has an ability to see the truth, and a great sense of honesty, level-headedness and logic. And, fool that she was, she loved me! There have been good times and bad, and yet there's always been something strong there to make it work.'

234

His recent declarations about love and marriage are nothing if not fervent.

My marriage vows are based on as long as we both shall love. I'm a family man above everything else. I believe in lust, I believe in romance, I believe in marriage. It's the time after the first infatuation that makes for real romance and a successful marriage. We tend to treat strangers better than we treat the person closest to us. In most marriages romance comes and goes like seasons. Perhaps we should all try a bit harder.

The callow, slightly selfish man who married Diandra in 1977 has developed into a more considerate and feeling person who sees his wife and son, not as a distraction from work but as the most important part of his life.

There cannot be many people who have a framed copy of their wedding vows in italic script on their office wall. Michael Douglas does, and the presence of that parchment commitment says a lot about the man. And yet he is still the man who can make the occasional reflective and sad comment, 'If your marriage is a constant burden, then you tend to think it might be nice to be alone.' Perhaps that deep and secret place within him to which so many people refer has never completely disappeared.

There is a strong feeling, a presentiment, of inevitable disaster. He is clearly aware that so much has gone right for him that some balancing out is inevitable. 'Providence, luck, good fortune, blessings. Whatever it is – I am actually scared sometimes even at my age that I should be prepared for some tragedy.'

Michael Douglas is certainly a popular man in the industry and fellow actors like Charlie Sheen testify to that fact. 'The guy is totally charming – and don't waste your time trying to find out he's not!' Sheen spent long periods with Douglas on and off-set while working on *Wall Street* and developed a strong regard for the man's personality and his talent. On several occasions Charlie Sheen admitted that 'Michael Douglas is the only actor I've met who is as dedicated and professional as my dad!' This wasn't pure sycophancy – one actor gushing over another – for Sheen's conflicts with Sean Young on *Wall Street* made headlines around the world. Sheen got to know Douglas during the course of research and filming, and his remarks are prompted by that developing friendship.

And the man who should know him better than any other can offer a slightly different picture. 'Oh, Michael's tough!' states Kirk Douglas. 'There's a piece of steel inside him. I just don't believe Michael is as sweet and charming as everyone says he is.'

That shy, nervous kid who followed his father onto the set of various spectacular movies has gone. In his place has appeared a relaxed, sophisticated, urbane socialite, able to talk equally effectively to actors and high finance tycoons.

He is a driven man. Obsessive about work, determined to bolt down every detail relating to production. This has often brought him into conflict with others working with, and for, him. Those conflicts can be stormy or even nasty, but it is to his great credit that the disputes are short-lived and entirely business-related. 'He doesn't bear a grudge. You have a row with him, sort it out, and later that night you'll be having a beer together and it's all forgotten,' stated one of his frequent crew members. 'He's a very straight guy.'

Despite his many successes, and the inevitable jealousy such triumphs create, there are no stories of virulent hatred of Michael Douglas. No stories like the one concerning Sharon Stone, his female lead in *Basic Instinct* who, filming in Africa earlier in her career was required to take a bath in a tub for one scene. Such was her popularity with cast and crew at the time that one crew member cheerfully relieved himself into the water just before her arrival.

Michael Douglas, the straight guy – Oscar winner, hugely powerful mogul, and sometime happy family man – is at the pinnacle of his profession, and it is unlikely that anything will shake that supremacy. The man has worked very hard to build a sustained career, and is now one of a select band of actors of his generation who are in constant demand by production and film companies. Joe Roth, shortly after taking over as chief of 20th Century Fox, stated, 'If you want to have some security about making a $50 million investment it would be very nice to have Danny De Vito, or Michael Douglas, or Robert Redford on the other end of that camera.'

He is fully aware of his importance in the film world and of what could happen to him in the years to come. 'I think there's an advantage in achieving success later in one's career. I've been doing this sort of thing for twenty years. I don't feel that fear. I was resigned after "Cuckoo's nest" to it being the highlight of my life, and look what's happened. I'm pretty proud of my résumé now. It stands up pretty well.' As the years go on the importance of *Cuckoo's Nest* to his career is receding as further triumphs and box-office smashes take their rightful place in his c.v. In an industry where you are only as hot as your last film he has done enough since *Cuckoo's Nest* to justify himself.

And maybe the most succinct comment on his career came when, being interviewed about his work on *Wall Street* he was asked if he was satisfied. After several seconds he replied, 'I don't think anybody is completely satisfied. If you are completely satisfied you have stopped living!'

But he is a man who will probably always be denied total happiness. He has achieved massive success in his professional life and enviable contentment in his private life but somehow it doesn't seem enough. 'I'm constantly under struggle. I'm constantly under the crazies, and part of the reason I work as much as I do is because of the crazies and to put them into a structured, positive light, rather than a destructive light,' he admitted gloomily. 'And I can see I go right to wrong, good to bad, good-bad, good-bad, and there's never an answer in sight!'

He seems obsessed with human frailties, and often admits that he looks for roles which allow him to explore the weaknesses in the human condition. 'I have an attraction to flawed characters. I don't believe in idyllic qualities. I've never had analysis or therapy, but I'm not proud of that – I wish I had a little bit better idea of what makes me tick,' he stated. 'I'd like to think my attraction to life's dark side has to do with a desire to dig for honesty, for truth – bursting bubbles until you get down and down, and then you realize there's a vicious side to all of us, a defensive side, a survival side. In society we try to conduct ourselves in a civilized manner, and I'm as good as anybody at it. But on the other side of that is a basic, carnal animal.'

'Michael's a much sweeter guy than I am, but underneath he has as much toughness,' commented his father. 'He's explosive, unpredictable!'

Unusually within the entertainment industry he is concerned by matters more substantial than his own ego. Traditionally the overwhelming concern of the hippie, current and ex, has been the human condition and Douglas has both the sensitivity and the intellectual capacity to handle such weighty concepts, even without the help of chemical stimulants. Many observers have been surprised by the incisiveness of his thoughts on issues of the day. This is not yet another narcissist, concerned only with his profile and reflection.

'I don't see a lot that makes sense in the world around me. I don't see many beautiful things,' admitted Douglas sadly. 'Things generally look confused and disturbed to me. By making movies or acting in them, it's a way of doing something.'

As an afterthought on the importance of acting, Michael Douglas, the man who recently received over $10 million for a single film, added, 'And it keeps the wolf from the door!'

He is also surprisingly open about his failings. 'I always knew in my heart that I'd be a late bloomer. Yeah, I would say it was only eight or ten years ago that I ceased to be scared of the camera,' he admitted. 'I've always struggled with confidence.'

His lack of security is a constant theme in his remarks. 'I really had no training, so maybe that's when I began to get cautious, out of fear, just not knowing what to do.'

Even the Oscar failed to deliver him from that surprising despair. The love of his wife and son have gone a long way to reinforcing his self-esteem but there is a void, an ache in Michael Douglas which will probably never be completely healed. The ragman's son begat the ragman's grandson and his abiding legacy was a mass of neuroses which are likely to afflict Michael Douglas for the whole of his life.

It is his primary achievement that he has climbed above the immediate effects of those psychological traumas. The Michael Douglas who bared all in *Basic Instinct* is a man at the top of his profession, with everything, in material terms, that anybody could desire. But above all his prizes and accolades and achievements he would probably be most proud of a simple comment from a family friend who has known the Douglas family since before Michael was born.

'Michael Douglas? Heck of a nice guy. Take the best parts of Kirk – drive, vigour, strength – then add the best parts of Diana – kindness, consideration, gentleness – and add something unique of his own, and there you've got Michael. A very special man!'

Even Julia Phillips' infamous swipe at Hollywood, *You'll Never Eat Lunch In This Town Again*, didn't attack or malign Douglas, which, for that book was unusual. Almost everybody else mentioned was slammed and slashed in her delicate prose.

In an industry not renowned for its generosity of spirit Michael Douglas is in a very special position. Respected and liked by his peers as someone who has worked his way up through the business. 'He's not just another rich kid living off his dad and his dad's name,' commented a studio insider. 'He's done the lot and deserves everything he's got!'

This would be a pleasing epitaph for most people and yet, fortunately, Michael Douglas is in no need for such a professional or private tribute yet. His complicated personal life and his demanding career both have a long way to run before *Variety* needs to compose a full assessment of Michael K. Douglas.

10   *The Top Bracket*

As he approaches his fiftieth year Michael Douglas is in a most enviable situation. He has achieved a position of eminence in his chosen profession, one of a handful of stars considered bankable by the independent forces which control so much in modern Hollywood. It is the level of fee which determines status and the $10 to 14 million for *Basic Instinct* put Douglas in that top bracket.

And his work in that film, plus others like *Fatal Attraction* and *Wall Street* demonstrate an essential truth about the man and his work. He has a widespread appeal across racial and gender restrictions. How many other actors in that mid-forties age group would have been able to generate the same intensity in the part of the possessed Nick Curran whilst not appearing ridiculous in the acrobatic sex scenes? A very limited bunch of names spring to mind and Michael Douglas doesn't suffer in comparison with any of them.

He has developed a career, from unpromising beginnings, to the point where he is now a member of that A-group of actors who can virtually write their own contracts. He is special to companies like Carolco because he has taken the time and trouble to study the business. He appreciates the need for budgets, the obligation to deliver on time, and he has also developed a vision way beyond the village which is Hollywood. As the film industry entered a new golden age in the eighties with the development of extra markets like cable, and video tape and video disc, so the opportunities open to production companies became even greater. The market has become truly global so that a modest success, or even a failure, in American cinemas can still prove to be a huge revenue earner once the extra sales and international sales are taken into account.

Carolco has become a major element in the film business by its astute pre-sell policy. The company made millions by pre-selling films like *Rambo* and *Total Recall* to overseas markets purely on the names of Schwarzenegger and Stallone. 'We make movies that compete with the major studios in the international market,' stated Thomas Levine of Carolco.

'They have to contain a big element – like Arnold or Sly or Mike Douglas – that is what lets us compete. So there's not that much quibbling about salaries.'

Perhaps his production work on *Cuckoo's Nest* first taught Douglas these important commercial lessons, but he has never forgotten. His appearance at Cannes for the 1992 Film Festival was ostensibly to promote *Basic Instinct* but was also part of his studied and constant involvement with the wider film world.

'For a lot of pictures foreign is larger and video is even larger. I spend time promoting my pictures overseas. That's why a company like Carolco knows it can sell its pictures in all those territories.'

To substantiate his point he willingly travelled to Cannes for the 1992 Film Festival to promote the controversial film along with Stone, Tripplehorn and Verhoeven. Promotion and marketing of films has always been one of his main concerns. In most of his successes he has been careful to identify some strong piece of promotion and use and exploit it to the betterment of the picture. Many other stars refuse to do this. Many other stars don't even consider it, but as Douglas is fond of saying, 'the picture comes first'.

However, he is also mercilessly aware of his own importance in this lucrative equation. Questioned about how he justified his *Basic Instinct* fee in the light of the wave of economies and cost-cuttings which hit Hollywood in recent years he snapped, 'Why should I give myself away? Just because you have a new austerity programme that has nothing to do with me. Life is not fair. If life were fair the studios would share video profits, the largest source of their income, on an equitable basis.'

This may sound a rather petty objection for Douglas to make but his words hint at a major change which has affected the film industry in recent years. In 1980 the proportionate income split between cinemas and ancillary sales was in the region 80:20. By the end of the decade it had completely reversed and was running at something like 25:75. A major film like *Batman* can take some $250 million in cinemas in its first few months of release but then earn some $400 million from video sales and rentals!

Figures like these account for Michael's legendary careful control of his due fees from film companies. There are often uneasy echoes of Kirk's continual railings against studios and studio accountants, but Michael, and before him his father, remains sure of his position and convinced that if he has a value to a production then the company setting up that production has to meet his valuation of his worth, otherwise he won't play. 'I'm sure you're thinking, "What can you say with the kind of money you make as an actor?" I defend myself with my credentials and with my success in foreign markets.'

Many years ago he realized that he was attracting massive interest overseas. 'The foreign markets took me under their wing before the States did!' As a result he now has a global bargaining power with companies like Carolco which makes him a very valuable property. Unpleasantly for various parties in Los Angeles who still yearn for the old days when people like actors knew their place, Michael Douglas will insist on getting every cent owing to him. And he knows the rules of the game sufficiently to ensure that he will get it.

He refuses to play the internecine games so beloved of Hollywood. He prefers, for family reasons, to live in either New York or in Santa Barbara when in the United States. With modern forms of travel there is no longer the need to live in the company town, as Los Angeles was for several decades. From Santa Barbara or New York he can be in Hollywood in a short time reducing the need to be constantly available.

This means a lot to him and to his wife and son. Diandra's problems with Hollywood are well documented but they left scars which she will not easily forget. Michael has no reason to feel affection for Hollywood or Los Angeles. In spirit and temperament, thanks to *Streets* and *Basic Instinct*, he has much more affinity with San Francisco, but he would not choose to live there either. His chosen absence from Los Angeles has put a further stamp on his reputation as a loner and a rebel. Many stars choose not to live in Los Angeles any longer. The days have gone when Beverly Hills was virtually a film-star village with actors and actresses kept in pampered luxury within calling distance of the studio lots. Douglas is not alone in his isolation but he seemed to attract more than his due share of criticism as an outsider.

Yet that is a description which has often seemed to follow him throughout his rollercoaster life in films. Even prior to his career in films, as a young man and a child, he had experienced the pain of feeling himself excluded. The damage such sensibilities inflicted upon him can only be imagined and there is a hurt and a vulnerability in his eyes which makes his various characterizations so appealing and convincing. The toughness and cruelty is always there but there is a sensitive edge which Kirk could never achieve.

That pain is deep-rooted and long-lasting. From the vivid rejection of his parents' divorce when he was a small child, through the regular isolation of being sent across America to be with whichever parent's turn it was, Michael Douglas suffered emotional scarring throughout his formative years. He withdrew into himself many years ago and though the barriers have been pulled down most of the way he is still concerned to keep at least part of himself private and secure.

Friendly, gregarious, popular – Douglas is all of these things and more but he is never going to be completely open. With all the hurts he has suffered who could blame him?

11   *The Head Man*

It is now twenty-five years since Michael Douglas took his first acting job. A quarter of a century in which he has achieved a unique position in the film world. He is a very well-respected actor able to pick and choose from a welter of scripts offered to him. More significantly he is in the top echelon of producers, a significant money-maker and that is truly the universal language in the film community. None of his more recent productions have matched the commercial success of *One Flew Over the Cuckoo's Nest* and yet the memory of the $200 million and more taken by the film is a powerful reminder.

So powerful that he has received a stream of offers to take a more proprietorial role in the industry. He has been asked three times to head major studios, but each time he has refused. Very probably his friends like Sherry Lansing and Dawn Steele advised him against any such bureaucratic move. As he commented, 'You lose all your friends. You have to feed this voracious machine. And what do I end up with? A producing deal? Some stock?'

Perhaps strangely he has not moved into directing films. Most other actors and actresses of his stature have found it difficult to resist the temptation of standing on the other side of the camera. Names as diverse as Clint Eastwood and Meryl Streep have indulged their talents as director. Michael Douglas has steadfastly refused despite the several approaches which have been made. He directed a couple of episodes of *Streets of San Francisco* and did a sound job but showed little interest in pursuing that side of the business.

Perhaps the reason for such distancing from the director's chair lies in his early involvement in producing. No other actor of his generation made such a stunning debut as a producer, and he clearly found that the work was something he liked and at which he excelled.

I love the fact that on one side, with acting, you can be a child – acting is wonderful for its innocence and the fun – and I think it helps you with producing.

On the other side, producing is fun for all the adult kinds of things you do. You deal with business, you deal with creative forces. As an adult who continues to get older, you like the adult risks. It's flying without a net, taking chances and learning. I was never good in economics or business – had no business background, you know – and I like it. By

250

producing you learn all these different things.

He made these remarks shortly before the release of *Jewel of the Nile*, but his starry progress since then demonstrates that his views have not altered.

In that light it shouldn't be surprising that he has steadfastly declined most invitations to direct. Although he was listed as assistant director on his father's film *The Heroes of Telemark* this was just a grandiose title for a gopher and a sycophantic sop to the star.

There are surely sufficient challenges for him as an actor and a producer, and yet his success in both those fields has caused people to question his motives. 'After *Cuckoo* people were surprised that I wanted to act. After *Wall Street* people were surprised that I wanted to produce.'

His work as a producer has brought him many plaudits, and his many admirers claim he is very unselfish in that role. 'A lot of actors who have production companies look to take the best roles for themselves. Probably my strength when I'm acting and producing is that I look to the best for the picture. You are very conscious of ego ramifications.'

Douglas is surprisingly candid when asked to explain the success of so many of his films. 'Honest to God I don't know. I think one aspect is that the movies with which I've been associated are good pictures. Beyond that I just don't know.

Quite honestly I never thought that I had the same magic that, say, Kathleen has – to jump out from the screen. I used to be envious of it. But as to my own appeal I'm not a very good judge of it.'

Many interviewers are intrigued by the question of what he considers to be his special appeal and it is one he faces regularly. On another occasion he admitted, 'I think it's the choice of material. It's also the ability to close your eyes and picture the movie. You can see it in your head and know if it's going to work or not.'

He is always conscious of the conflict between his roles as actor and producer. 'I've always been an actor first, but there's not a lot of good parts around – that's a lot of why I've immersed myself in producing.'

To another interviewer he snapped, 'Look, I don't just produce. I also like to act. I'm an actor first and a producer second!'

That conflict can be misinterpreted by some people. 'I have never been the first choice of a lot of good directors. There's a certain resentment of an actor who has a producing background. It makes directors uncomfortable,' admitted Douglas. 'Some of them think you may be second guessing them even if you're not. And producing is sometimes perceived as a lack of obsession about acting.'

One of the highest compliments paid to Douglas is that he is invariably a popular man on-set, and this does not refer just to his famous punch-up with a certain autocratic director! Invariably people within the industry like him because of his sheer professionalism.

There is a common perception that his involvement in a film means a solid quality job being delivered on time and invariably on budget. There are few stories of high-handed tantrums surrounding Michael Douglas, unlike many of his contemporaries. A member of the crew on *Romancing* and *Jewel* commented, 'He always gets the respect of his peers because people can see that he's paid his dues. Respect comes from the lads on the shop floor, the carpenters and so on, not just the Lansings and Spielbergs.'

Douglas is clearly aware of the possible conflicts caused by his dual role on films like *Romancing*. 'Being a producer/actor is awkward for people. They don't know how to deal with you,' he admits. 'You've hired everybody who does everything. You've signed the contracts. People don't like to applaud the employer.'

James Bridges, director of *The China Syndrome*, was in a special position to see Douglas acting and producing in the same film. 'It's not always easy working with an actor who's also the producer. At first I was a bit intimidated. I had to direct the boss. But Michael didn't bring his acting role into his producing role, or vice versa.'

'I love my work and I'm really fortunate. It's an adult sandbox. It's make-believe,' stated Douglas after *Romancing* was finished. 'It allows you to learn about mental hospitals or nuclear power plants or to travel all over the jungle and meet charming and attractive and sexy people. It's a wonderful circus life, and I couldn't conceive of doing anything else.'

'Acting is like being a child and producing is like being an adult,' admitted Douglas. 'It's a magical combination of activities!'

He attracts deep respect within the industry for his willingness to put the film first rather than his own interests. 'I think that's paid off in my feature successes,' he admitted. 'Not so much for being singled out for the great performance, but because the cumulative effect is my movies are good!' Actresses like Glenn Close, Kathleen Turner, and Sharon Stone could endorse this view as each of them have crashed into the big league as a direct result of working with the remarkably unselfish Michael Douglas.

He states his thoughts on his historical role in a typically forthright way. 'Look, I've got a healthy ego. And we all have our own ways and styles of approaching things. The best, most satisfying way for me is to make the best picture.'

Michael Douglas is obviously happy about being a simple actor on a film. With films that he is not producing he can relax rather more. The only responsibility is to show up and do the business. 'I love being an actor for hire. No one cherishes that more than I do!'

His love of acting comes across very strongly,

but he is aware of and concerned by the schizophrenia involved in his dual role. 'In acting you're paid to be selfish. Producing you have to have three hundred and sixty degree vision. I don't know if producing affects my acting; I know it makes acting less fun.'

In a peculiar way Douglas became typecast as a producer very early in his career, and has occasionally found it difficult to throw off that label. 'After I got out of the TV series and produced *Cuckoo's Nest* there was this false image that I wasn't interested in acting any more, but I was.'

Plaintively he bemoans the problems which beset him as a major actor in Hollywood. 'There just don't seem to be the parts around. I love acting, and I want to do more, but I can't find the roles and when I do there's always a lot of competition for them.'

He describes the difficulties of being both producer and actor by recalling incidents during the shoot on *Jewel*. 'I'd be in the middle of a love scene with Kathleen and a production assistant would come in and say, "Michael, we've got this problem", and I'd have to turn round to Kathleen and say, "Uh Kathleen, can you wait a moment?" '

One of his major qualities as an actor and a producer is the ability to recognize his strengths and weaknesses. 'I think I'm a good logician. The art of logic is reducing everything to the lowest common denominator, and I think I have a good ability to see what the priorities are,' he admitted.

'I think that my biggest strength is instinct. I feel like I'm really lucky. I have good instincts, and I trust them. My first instinct is right a large amount of the time. And when I get into a bind I try to remember what my first instinct was in the situation and go with that.'

He also recognizes the darker side to his personality. 'I try to be diplomatic. But if it gets ugly, I'll mix it up with anybody. I've got no problems with that at all. And I do, on occasions. It's not my style, but if I've got to, I do it. I didn't get this far just from being a nice guy.'

His reputation as an affable, pleasant individual is not totally deserved. 'I'm not always a nice guy. A number of film studios turned me down on *Cuckoo's Nest*. And some of these same men also turned down *The China Syndrome*. They really fucked around with me. Well, I keep tabs. I'll get even. But in the meantime, I'm getting great satisfaction.'

His commitment to projects has become legendary in the business. 'I don't just put together a deal and walk away. I stay with a production. And I think I'm a pretty good sounding board for people. I never take a domineering role. Some producers like making deals. I like making movies.' Many of his peers enjoy being in the business because of the money and the power, and attendant rewards, they provide. Michael Douglas is in the business primarily because he likes films and making them. He also enjoys the very good life provided by his status but it is the hands-on involvement in filming which is most crucial.

Producer Polly Platt has worked with Douglas on several projects and has deep respect for his ability and his personality. 'Jesus, God, what a gentleman! He is very canny about money and he knows how to get it – all of it. The only thing that he was really hard about was getting his overtime. Actually as he was a producer I thought maybe he was going to give me a break!'

He didn't set out to be a producer or a businessman. It was acting which was the draw even in those balmy days in the Californian hills. Back then he could only dream of achieving a fraction of his father's success; now he can justifiably claim that he has nothing to prove. The legend which was Kirk Douglas, Hollywood star, was a major obstacle round Michael's neck for many years. He struggled for years to shake off the awesome weight of his father's reputation. Once he had created his own place in the spotlight he was at last able to speak objectively about the problems which being the son of Spartacus brought to his life:

As he recently commented:

It's great to play a part which they compare to the best your father's done. I'm a tremendous fan of his; he's got twelve performances that are classics. But I didn't try to be a clone. Now people say, 'Oh, he does have that quality his dad has, but he can also do light comedy, he can do sensitive young men, he can do action pictures, he can do killer guys.' Suddenly you've worked yourself up to the top of the pecking order, and you say to yourself, okay, this is going to be fun . . .

It would be easy for him to deny or minimize the importance of his father in providing a grounding in the business but he will not appear so churlish.

I spent my summers with my father or went on location with him. And I could see how he handled himself. His business is and was being a movie star as well as a producer. I saw him at parties with other stars. I saw them as real people trying to conduct their lives in some sort of health despite the tension. Those things were the real strength of being brought up in the business.

He also learned many valuable lessons about the business from Kirk, particularly the value of independent production. In the forties and fifties Kirk Douglas had achieved a position of dominance within the industry by effectively bucking the system. Despite being advised against it by a number of 'experts' Kirk insisted on forming his own companies and channelling projects through them. Bryna, named after his mother, was the most prominent and through Bryna he was able to become and thrive independently of the main body of the film business. Following his lead Michael began his own production wing in 1972 and has continued on that lucrative and fulfilling course ever since.

Unlike many others in a similar position he is not slow to praise his father for his influence.

> A mentor is an important part of any career. I consider my father a mentor. He has incredible stamina – tenacity, endurance – and you need that for a picture. He taught me that you do the best you can, and then you walk away from it. The biggest advantage of being second generation is that it keeps you grounded. You see your father's foibles and insecurities – not what the public sees. I think it's helped me handle my successes and my failures.

Those failures have been many and have helped him keep a sense of perspective on the business. In his résumé for every *Wall Street* or *Basic Instinct* there is a *Napoleon and Samantha* or *Shining Through*, and when his position in film history is finally determined it will almost certainly be distinguished by more than his fair share of turkeys.

His first significant production company was Bigstick and that initial venture with Bigstick grew into a multi-million dollar business empire. Chrome and tinted glass offices eventually became an elegant front for excursions into property and real estate. After several lucrative approaches he decided to form a completely fresh company.

Stonebridge Entertainment was the name of the new organization, and a deal was quickly struck with Dawn Steele's Columbia Pictures. The terms of the deal were remarkably similar to those established in the earlier production deal between Bigstick and Columbia, but was even more solid thanks to the incursions of the Sony Corporation into Hollywood.

Douglas formed the new company as a partnership with Rick Bieber, previously head of production at Home Box Office Pictures. Bieber was enthusiastic and idealistic and had established a glowing reputation within the industry. He had been responsible for initiating a sensitive biography of Nelson Mandela, and he had also produced an award-winning study of American Neo-Nazis.

Bieber began with high hopes for Stonebridge. 'There are plans to move into music publishing, recording and singing talent, of building a small conglomerate.' The company began searching out projects and earmarked a horror movie starring Kiefer Sutherland to be followed by a hard-living cop film starring Kathleen Turner.

Stonebridge made its debut with the film, *Flatliners*, which proved an immediate success for the company. It cost a mere $16 million and took in well over $150 million. However, other early Stonebridge projects fared not so well. *Stone Cold*, *Double Impact* and *Hard Promises* suffered in comparison and receipts were poor. The next Stonebridge production, *Radio Flyer*, received critical acclaim but failed to set any income columns afire.

That initial project from the divinely inspired Guber-Peters team was an ambitious and courageous treatment of the serious theme of child molestation, but failed to register with the audiences.

The clear failure of the film left the production company a rather pasty-faced infant. The various difficulties were heightened by the fact that in three of those four films the director had to be replaced after shooting had commenced.

Such problems led Douglas to re-evaluate his involvement with Stonebridge. 1991 had been a difficult year for him. The work on *Shining Through* and then *Basic Instinct* was gruelling and demanding, and he didn't need, nor want, the worries caused by the obvious lack of progress with Stonebridge, despite the important support from Columbia.

The partnership arrangement with Rick Bieber terminated at the end of 1991, and Douglas began an intensive overhaul of the company. In effect this resulted in a severe pruning of the company's activities. Many staff were released and the company is now a much smaller, tighter organization with Douglas the unquestioned and unchallenged head. He still seeks the total involvement of production but the revamping of Stonebridge means that he will not be undertaking any such tasks unless and until he finds a project which will provide him with complete satisfaction. But projects like *One Flew Over the Cuckoo's Nest* may only come along once in a lifetime. Douglas has been incredibly fortunate in that respect once; surely it couldn't happen again?

Michael Douglas now lives the life of the rich sybarite choosing when and where and with whom to work. Houses in New York and Santa Barbara plus a ranch in Aspen, Colorado and a villa in Majorca are but part of his property interests. The palatial Santa Barbara house has become the main family residence since 1990, and Michael and Diandra are busily renovating the house to suit its breathtaking setting. The couple feel that the Santa Barbara location will provide Cameron, plus any possible brother or sister, with the space and the freshness to grow healthily. Immersing himself in the Hollywood maelstrom has never been important to Michael Douglas, and he obviously wants to keep Cameron away from the many pressures of Los Angeles, if possible.

'And I think our choice of living in Santa Barbara, California, or in New York and staying out of the industry mainstream is going to help a lot – it's helped me!'

The Douglas family at play has the time and

financial security to indulge themselves in any exotic locations they choose, but invariably base themselves for vacations around one of their houses.

The family side of his life has apparently settled down into a comfortable accommodation between the couple. There are even thoughts about a second child, a brother or sister for Cameron who is now a teenager. 'We're thinking about it – if you could promise me a girl,' laughed Douglas. 'I'm a bit nervous about going into my sixties with some boy wanting to play ball. But give me a little girl on my knee and I'd be very happy!

'We've celebrated our fifteenth anniversary, and we were actually commenting the other day on how good we felt and how we were looking forward to the future,' commented Douglas proudly.

That future is rich with promise, and there is no predicting what dizzy heights he might reach as actor or producer, or even director over the next decade. Yet there are also intriguing possibilities of a sensational move into a totally different direction. There have been a number of overtures to him to make a complete career shift sideways into politics. When he began his acting career the idea of an actor going into politics was treated with justifiable ridicule. The intervening years, and Ronald Reagan, have changed all that.

Michael Douglas has had subtle approaches

from both parties, and is clearly considering the attraction of a political career. Given his proven organizational ability, and the obvious sharpness of his mind, there would be few people who would doubt his chances to succeed. And more than one interviewer has noted Michael's politician-like ability to astutely deflect a worrying or intrusive question.

The only problem might be Michael's colourful past. His drug involvement, and wild lifestyle would certainly be used against him by political enemies, but he may be prepared to take that chance.

A generation ago the thought of a mere actor reaching the highest political office of all was too laughable to even consider. One of the early director colleagues of Michael Douglas even wrote that scenario into a major film script. One of the biggest jokes in Robert Zemeckis' *Back to the Future* came when Marty McFly, having travelled back thirty years to 1955, was trying to convince the mad professor that he had come from the future. Asked to name the President in the mid-eighties he replies 'Ronald Reagan' and is greeted with derisive laughter.

Yet Ronald Reagan did make it to the Presidency and became the most popular President ever in the polls. Following that bizarre development there is no reason to believe that the infinitely more talented and more personable Michael Douglas couldn't continue that tradition.

He would be a much more marketable proposition than the haggard Reagan. The image of an active, purposeful man as fostered in *China Syndrome*, *Romancing* and *Black Rain* would complement the sex symbol image created by *Fatal Attraction* and *Basic Instinct*. In several respects Douglas already has a potential constituency and party bosses are obviously aware of his potential as a dynamic, Kennedy-type figure. His still-boyish charm, comfortable way with the media, and demonstrably easy manner of making speeches are all major attractions for the two parties.

He cuts an impressive figure, whether in the sharp, Gordon Gekko attire or in his more favoured casual clothing. His hair is now streaked with silver giving him a distinguished, magisterial appearance, and in a political system which is growing ever more presidential, Michael Douglas would be an immense capture for either party.

He takes risks by expressing opinions on political matters which are difficult to imagine escaping from many other personalities' mouths. In the run-up to the Primary season in America he voiced exasperation with the ease with which his profession was used by politicians. His remarks seemed to be provoked by the sight of Arnold Schwarzenegger cavorting behind George Bush in New Hampshire. 'We actors tend to be really suckers. We lend our names to politicians who make a lot of money and we never ask a lot in return.'

He also took the time to articulate his feelings on the presidential race in 1992. 'I'm not supporting anyone this time. I'm disappointed in the field. There is no real leader. Television is making personalities more important than ideas.'

He would be a prize catch for either Republicans or Democrats, and the media circus which would follow his announcing his candidature can only be imagined. The sight of Michael Douglas making a keynote speech at a party caucus or even a Convention would attract television coverage from all over the world, and no party boss would pass up the chance for such free publicity for the party.

There is also a real element of heroism to compensate for the fake derring-do of such swashbuckling epics as *Romancing the Stone*. During location shooting in San Francisco on *Streets* a dreadful accident happened to one of the stunt men when a powerboat mowed him down during filming. Who was it who dived into the water to save him? None other than film star and possible candidate Michael K. Douglas.

'The water all round him was turning red. The next thing I knew, I was in the water – fully clothed – swimming towards him. It was just an instinctive reaction on my part.' Stunt man Robert Butler stated, 'Without Mike's prompt action I'm sure I'd never have made it. I'll forever be grateful to him for saving my life.' A presidential citation for bravery was the reward for Michael Douglas and it is not difficult to predict the way the image-makers would use that incident in any future campaign.

The likely model for Michael Douglas, John Fitzgerald Kennedy, made great capital from his alleged heroics on his wartime navy boat PT-109, and the courage of Michael Douglas, as demonstrated in the saving of Robert Butler's life, would almost certainly be milked to equally good effect. It is not difficult to anticipate him moving on to a political stage. He has never been afraid to become involved in political or environmental issues, often to his own short term disadvantage. His occasional moves into such areas as publishing betray a social concern which cries out for further realization, and many of his 'concerns' are part of the general liberal tradition of American politics.

He has a long-established reputation as a champion of assorted liberal causes. In the wake of the murder of John Lennon in 1980 Douglas founded, in association with Jann Wenner, the publisher of *Rolling Stone*, the National Alliance Against Violence. In 1991 he created the Michael Douglas Foundation to channel money, much of it being his own, into various charitable projects. A number of other works, some in conjunction with Diandra, prove that there is a compassionate humanitarian beneath the Hollywood exterior. Many of his comments relate to a world beyond the film camera, and politics, particularly the

American variety, needs intelligent, sensitive candidates.

And yet it would be impossible to maintain any kind of career in entertainment whilst simultaneously running seriously for office. The charges of frivolous behaviour are easy to imagine and the party bosses would insist on a complete divorce from acting and producing as the basic charge for a ticket. His many comments on making films show that it isn't just a job or a professional commitment. 'You can't help yourself – it's like falling in love. So I have to do it; it's like I can't control it!'

The man has a deep and intuitive love for the whole process of making films, from arranging finance through to overseeing the daily production chores, acting and starring in films, and even controlling the promotion and merchandising of the finished product. It would be hard emotionally for him to divorce himself from the glittering world which has been all he has known for most of his life.

And yet he has an obvious and rather endearing sense of his own value in the greater scale of things. 'Think of it, here are people like my father and me who are getting paid to give all day long, to be charming and funny and sexy to the public. Reporters follow you around taking down your words. You get a false sense of importance. Then you go home and the kids won't listen to you and you wind up screaming your head off because you are not getting that same kind of attention!'

Douglas has an endearing, and, for his profession, rare grasp of the fact that the world doesn't revolve around him, whether as an individual or a star. He could leave show business without suffering major damage to his ego system.

Moving into politics wouldn't harm him financially. His first real money, from *Streets of San Francisco*, enabled him to take the time to produce *Cuckoo's Nest*. That project made him a multi-millionaire, and proceeds from other films have made Michael Douglas very, very wealthy. He has been in the major league for fees for films for several years. Even in the new era of austerity currently being experienced in Hollywood any Michael Douglas signature on a contract requires the presence of several noughts before ink touches the page.

Although entering politics would not harm him financially some may suspect that he would miss the ego-satisfaction of appearing in films and television and, at one time, on stage. Like most film stars Douglas finds the adulation coming from his position both exciting and intoxicating.

It might be hard to forgo the buzz he always gets from acting and appearing on chat shows and being interviewed. And yet what Hollywood film could compare with the potency of 1600 Pennsylvania Avenue.

Few people who know the man would place odds against Michael Douglas entering politics at a mayoral level, like Clint Eastwood or Sonny Bono, or even as a state governor, or member of Congress. One of the advertising men behind Reagan's campaigns commented, 'Hell, we could get a monkey elected if we had enough bucks behind the campaign!'

Perhaps that man proved his point in his subsequent work for Ronald Reagan. However, Michael Douglas has so much more going for him than the previous President that it seems inevitable that at some point he will elect to run. Given his record of triumphing against all the odds it would be a brave man to deny his chances of ultimate political success.

President Douglas, sometime in the early twenty-first century? It has a definite ring to it, and what an achievement it would be for Kirk Douglas to see his son, the ragman's grandson, at the top of the pile?

Filmography

HAIL, HERO! (1969)
Producer: Harold D. Cohen. *Director*: David Miller. *Cast*: Arthur Kennedy, Michael Douglas, Teresa Wright, John Larch, Charles Drake, Peter Strauss. *Screenplay*: Based on a novel by John Weston.
A Cinema Centre Film/Halcyon Production
National General

ADAM AT 6AM (1970)
Producer: Cinema Centre (uncredited). *Director*: Robert Scheerer. *Cast*: Michael Douglas, Lee Purcell, Joe Don Baker, Grayson Hall, Charles Aidman, Meg Foster.
Screenplay: Stephen and Elinor Karpf.
A Cinema Centre Film Production

SUMMERTREE (1971)
Producer: Kirk Douglas. *Director*: Anthony Newley. *Cast*: Michael Douglas, Barbara Bel Geddes, Jack Warden, Brenda Vaccaro, Kirk Callaway, Bill Vint. *Screenplay*: Based on Ron Cowan's off-Broadway play.
A Bryna Production
Columbia Pictures

WHEN MICHAEL CALLS (1971)
(Made for television)
Producer: Gil Shiva. *Director*: Philip Leacock. *Cast*: Ben Gazzara, Michael Douglas, Elizabeth Ashley, Karen Pearson, Albert S. Waxman. *Screenplay*: James Bridges (based on a novel by John Farris).
A Palomar Pictures International Production
20th Century Fox

NAPOLEON AND SAMANTHA (1972)
Producer: Walt Disney Productions. *Director*: Bernard McEveety. *Cast*: Michael Douglas, Jodie Foster, Henry Jones, Will Greer, Johnny Whittaker, Arch Johnson, Ellen Corby. *Screenplay*: Stewart Raffill.
Walt Disney Productions

STREETS OF SAN FRANCISCO (1972)
(Made for television, pilot for series)
Producer: Quinn Martin. *Cast*: Karl Malden, Michael Douglas, Robert Wagner, Kim Darby, John Rubinstein, Tom Bosley, Andrew Duggan, Edward Andrews, Mako. *Screenplay*: Ed Hume (based on Carolyn Weston's *Poor, Poor Ophelia*).
A Quinn Martin Production

COMA (1978)
Producer: Martin Erlichman. *Director*: Michael Crichton. *Cast*: Genevieve Bujold, Michael Douglas, Tom Selleck, Elizabeth Ashley, Rip Torn, Richard Widmark, Lois Chiles, Lance LeGault. *Screenplay*: Michael Crichton (based on Robin Cook's novel)
MGM

THE CHINA SYNDROME (1979)
Producer: Michael Douglas. *Director*: James Bridges. *Cast*: Jack Lemmon, Jane Fonda, Michael Douglas, Scott Brady, James Hampton, Peter Donat, Wilford Brimley, James Karen, Diandra Morrell (Douglas). *Screenplay*: James Bridges, Mike Gray, T.S. Cook.
A Michael Douglas/IPC Films Presentation
Columbia Pictures

RUNNING (1979)
Producers: Robert Cooper and Ronald Cohen. *Director*: Steven Hilliard Stern. *Cast*: Michael Douglas, Susan Anspach, Lawrence Dane, Philip Akin, Eugene Levy, Charles Shamata. *Screenplay*: Steven Hilliard Stern.
Universal

IT'S MY TURN (1980)
Producer: Martini Elfand. *Director*: Claudia Weill. *Cast*: Jill Clayburgh, Michael Douglas, Beverly Garland, Charles Grodin, Steven Hill, Teresa Baxter, John Gabriel, Joan Copeland. *Screenplay*: Eleanor Bergstein.
Columbia Pictures

THE STAR CHAMBER (1983)
Producer: Frank Yablans. *Director*: Peter Hyams. *Cast*: Michael Douglas, Yaphet Kotto, Hal Holbrook, Joe Regalbuto, Sharon Gless, James B. Sikking, Diana Dill, DeWayne Jessie, Don Calfa, Jack Kehoe. *Screenplay*: Peter Hyams and Roderick Taylor.
20th Century Fox

ROMANCING THE STONE (1984)
Producer: Michael Douglas. *Director*: Robert Zemeckis. *Cast*: Michael Douglas, Kathleen Turner, Danny De Vito, Alfonso Arau, Zack Norman, Holland Taylor, Manuel Ojeda. *Screenplay*: Raynold Gideon and Bruce Evans.
Columbia Pictures

A CHORUS LINE (1985)
Producers: Cy Feuer and Ernest Martin. *Director*: Richard Attenborough. *Cast*: Michael Douglas, Alyson Reed, Terrence Mann, Greg Burge, Cameron English, Vicki Frederick, Nicole Fosse, Audrey Landers, Janet Jones. *Screenplay*: Arnold Schulman (based on the original stage play).
Columbia Pictures

THE JEWEL OF THE NILE (1985)
Producer: Michael Douglas. *Director*: Lewis Teague. *Cast*: Kathleen Turner, Michael Douglas, Danny De Vito, Avner Eisenberg, Spiros Focas, Holland Taylor, The Flying Karamazov Brothers. *Screenplay*: Mark Rosenthal and Lawrence Konner.
20th Century Fox

FATAL ATTRACTION (1987)
Producers: Stanley Jaffe and Sherry Lansing. *Director*: Adrian Lyne. *Cast*: Michael Douglas, Glenn Close, Anne Archer. *Screenplay*: James Dearden.
Paramount Pictures

WALL STREET (1987)
Producer: Edward R. Pressman. *Director*: Oliver Stone. *Cast*: Michael Douglas, Charlie Sheen, Darryl Hannah, Martin Sheen, Terence Stamp, Sean Young, Hal Holbrook, Sylvia Miles. *Screenplay*: Stanley Weisner and Oliver Stone.
20th Century Fox

BLACK RAIN (1989)
Producers: Stanley Jaffe and Sherry Lansing. *Director*: Ridley Scott. *Cast*: Michael Douglas, Ken Takakura, Andy Garcia, Yusaka Matsuda, John Spencer, Shigeru Komaya, Stephen Root, Guto Ishimatsu, Tomisaburo Wakayama. *Screenplay*: Craig Bolotin and Warren Lewis.
Paramount/UIP

WAR OF THE ROSES (1989)
Producers: James L. Brooks and Arnon Milchan. *Director*: Danny DeVito. *Cast*: Michael Douglas, Kathleen Turner, Danny DeVito, Marianne Sagebrecht, Sean Astin, G.D. Spradlin, Heather Fairchild, Peter Donat, Dan Castellaneta, Gloria Cromwell, Susan Isaacs, Jacqueline Cassell. *Screenplay*: Michael Leeson (based on novel by Warren Adler).
20th Century Fox

SHINING THROUGH (1991)
Producers: Sandy Gallin, Howard Rosemann and Carol Baum. *Director*: David Seltzer. *Cast*: Melanie Griffith, Michael Douglas, Liam Neeson, Sir John Gielgud, Joely Richardson. *Screenplay*: David Seltzer.
20th Century Fox

BASIC INSTINCT (1991)
Producer: Allan Marshall. *Director*: Paul Verhoeven. *Cast*: Michael Douglas, Sharon Stone, George Dzundza, Jeanne Tripplehorn, Leilani Sarelli. *Screenplay*: Joe Eszterhas.
Carolco/TriStar

274

NON-APPEARING INVOLVEMENTS
IN FILMS

LONELY ARE THE BRAVE (1962)
(gopher and part-time film editor)

THE HEROES OF TELEMARK (1965)
Assistant Director

CAST A GIANT SHADOW (1966)
Production Assistant

ONE FLEW OVER THE CUCKOO'S NEST (1976)
Produced by Michael Douglas and Saul Zaentz

STARMAN (1984)
Produced by Michael Douglas

Index

279